# Third Person

First published in Italian as *Terza Persona* © Giulio Einaudi s.p.a, 2007

This English edition © Polity Press, 2012

Polity Press
65 Bridge Street
Cambridge CB2 1UR, UK

Polity Press
350 Main Street
Malden, MA 02148, USA

ISBN-13: 978-0-7456-4397-7
ISBN-13: 978-0-7456-4398-4(pb)

A catalogue record for this book is available from the British Library.

Typeset in 11 on 13 pt Sabon
by Toppan Best-set Premedia Limited

The publisher has used its best endeavours to ensure that the URLs for external websites referred to in this book are correct and active at the time of going to press. However, the publisher has no responsibility for the websites and can make no guarantee that a site will remain live or that the content is or will remain appropriate.

Every effort has been made to trace all copyright holders, but if any have been inadvertently overlooked the publisher will be pleased to include any necessary credits in any subsequent reprint or edition.

For further information on Polity, visit our website: www.politybooks.com

The translation of this work has been funded by SEPS
Segretariato Europeo per le Pubblicazioni Scientifiche

Via Val d'Aposa 7 – 40123 Bologna – Italy
seps@seps.it – www.seps.it

# Contents

# Introduction

1

If there is an unquestioned assumption in contemporary debate, it involves the value universally awarded to the category of person. No matter what the discipline – philosophy, theology, or one of the more specialized fields, like law or bioethics – personhood remains the basis for legitimizing every 'theoretically correct' discourse. This is not some well-reasoned conceptual choice. It is a given, one that apparently requires no further proof. Regardless of the starting perspective, it is hardly even conceivable today to take a critical look at what Maria Zambrano defined, back in the 1950s, as "the part of human life that is most alive, the living core capable of passing through biological death."[1] Although this assumption has been oriented toward different contexts of understanding and tied to a variety of definitions, it has never lost force, even during the waning of the 'personalist' movement. Quite the opposite: during the decline of personalism the paradigm of the person actually attracted renewed interest. As Paul Ricoeur announced some years back: "Death to personalism; long live the person!" While personalism "was not competitive enough to win the conceptual battle," the concept of person "remains the best candidate for the juridical, political, economic and social battles of our time."[2] The idea of person, whose most sophisticated inspiration came

from a specific branch of early nineteenth-century phenomenology,[3] was relaunched with ever greater intensity from this point
on. But it was an idea that cut across the entire face of contemporary philosophy,[4] spanning both analytic and continental philosophy as well as Catholic and secular schools of thought.

This convergence between Catholics and secularists – one that
has never been openly declared and is actually often denied, even
though the effects of its meaning are clearly at work – is easily
recognizable in the often bitterly polemical debate that, for over
twenty years, has regularly flared up on the slippery terrain of
bioethics. The debate hinges on determining the exact moment
when a living being – or on defining what type of living being –
can be considered a person, but never on the decisive value that
this attribution entails. Whether a life is declared to be personal
from the act of conception, at a certain stage of embryonic development, or from the moment of birth, its entrance into the regime
of personhood is what lends it unquestionable value. It hardly
matters whether one becomes a person by divine decree, through
natural means, all at once, or in a series of stages: what counts is
the threshold beyond which something generically living takes on
a significance that radically changes its legal status. Nowhere to
my knowledge, not even in the midst of the most profound dis-
agreement on what may or should be defined as a person (not to
mention the equally problematic distinction between a potential
and an actual person),[5] is what we, by habit or choice, call 'person'
ever questioned – much less its absolute onto-theological primacy.
If a tacit point of tangency exists between the seemingly opposing
conceptions of the Christian sacredness of life and the secular
notion of its quality, it resides precisely in this assumed superiority
of the personal over the impersonal: only a life that can provide
the credentials of personhood can be considered sacred or qualitatively significant.

When we turn from the lexicon of philosophy or bioethics to
the more defined lexicon of the law, not only do we find the same
assumption, we also recognize its conceptual roots. These lie in
the association, which the modern legal notion has made for some
time now, between the category of person and the subject of law,
tying them together in such a way as to make of the former a
condition for conceiving of the latter and vice versa. In order to

be able to assert what we call subjective rights – to life, to well-being, to dignity – we must first enter into the enclosed space of the person. Conversely, in a similar fashion, to be a person means to enjoy these rights in and of themselves. A recent formulation of this idea, picked up by a wide variety of writers, makes a claim for "the vindication of the right of every human being 'to have rights,' that is, to be a legal person, entitled to certain inalienable rights, regardless of the status of their political membership."[6] In these sorts of assertions there is more than the simple truism they appear to contain – namely that every human being must be considered as such. What we have here is the increasingly wide-spread idea that the category of person has the conceptual (and therefore, sooner or later, also practical) function of bridging the still dramatically gaping chasm between the concept of human being and that of citizen, set out so starkly by Hannah Arendt at the close of the Second World War. While she traced the origin of this gap to the failure to extend citizenship to – or to the willful removal of citizenship from – entire groups of people who were thus driven into the unendurable condition of statelessness, the attitude that takes shape with the 1948 Declaration of Rights is that it can only be filled by a notion endowed with a higher degree of universality than the modern concept of citizenship. From this conviction, one that is so established by now as to be considered implicit, was born the continually repeated call – or desire – to move away from the notion of individual to that of person, as expressed by the title of an influential study by Martha Nussbaum.[7]

Turning to specialized jurists, this position is further articulated along two apparently divergent vectors of meaning, which nevertheless find common ground in their shared agreement regarding the strategic importance of the person. Because of its universal applicability, personhood is seen as the only semantic field that can possibly overlap the two spheres of law and humanity, separated as they are by the national ideology of citizenship. This means that a concept like that of human rights is only conceivable and viable through the lexicon of personhood. As far as Luigi Ferrajoli is concerned, this does not mean negating the specificity of other types of rights, such as public rights granted only to citizens or political rights reserved only to those among them who are "capable of acting"; rather it means including all rights within a larger circle, constituted by the fundamental rights attributed to all the human beings endowed with the status of person. As the dynamics of globalization are breaking up the confines of national borders, driving legal praxis into increasingly international venues, human rights are no longer extended "to individuals because they are citizens, but rather, because they are persons."[8] This idea is bolstered, albeit in a different theoretical context, by Stefano Rodotà: he infers the renewed importance of the concept of person (which in his opinion, too, is destined to take the place of the more limited one of citizen) on the basis of the centrality of the body in the practical reality of actual conditions of existence. In this case "the shift in attention from the individual to the person, shown by the prevalence of this word in much of recent literature,"[9] is not due to its greater degree of abstraction, but rather to the fact that the term adheres more closely to the material situation of the living individual. While in the past practical conditions of life were excluded from the formal conception of the individual subject of law, today "we stand before a connection between humanity and law that takes the form of an interpenetration between person and fundamental rights."[10] To sum up: in this case, too, the category of person appears to be the only one that can unite human beings and citizens, body and soul, law and life.

## 2

But is this really how things stand? A quick look at the world situation raises a number of doubts on this point: the growing number of deaths from hunger, war, and epidemics is an eloquent testimony to the ineffectiveness of what has come to be called 'human rights.' If this phrase was intended to signal the inclusion of all human life within the protective space of the law, we are forced to admit that no right is less guaranteed today than the right to life. How can this be? Considering that the inviolability of the person has become the guiding light of all democratically inspired social theories, where does this widening divergence between the affirmation of the principle and its practical application originate? Was the category of the person not supposed to establish a definitive point of union between law and life, subjectivity and body, form and existence? Of course, one can always answer, as people often do, that the category has not been extended enough to produce the desired results, or that it has been only partially affirmed in terms of quantity, and only approximately in terms of quality. In spite of the idea of person being proclaimed, appealed to, and raised high on every banner, it has not taken firm root at the heart of interhuman relations.

The response offered in the following pages takes a different, even opposite, direction. The hypothesis that arises from this book, a more disturbing one altogether, is that the essential failure of human rights, their inability to restore the broken connection between rights and life, does not take place in spite of the affirmation of the ideology of the person but rather *because* of it. In other words, the failure of human rights is not to be conceptually traced to the limited extension of the ideology of the person but rather to its expansion; not to the fact that we have yet to enter fully into its regime of meaning, but to the fact that we have never really moved out of it. Of course this overly succinct, even intentionally drastic formulation anticipates a conclusion that will be presented in this book in a far more detailed and dialectical fashion. For one thing, as we shall see, the category of person is so inherently complex that it is not easily reducible to a single order of meaning. This is evident from the start, in its constitutive oscillation between the language of theology and the lexicon of the law – a duality that persists in the two registers through which its meaning is expressed today: the Catholic and the secular. But hermeneutic caution is equally suggested by another, perhaps even more significant consideration, this time of a historical nature. I am referring to the fact that when the category of person was relaunched at the end of the Second World War, it took form as an almost obligatory retort to the out-and-out attack it was subjected to – from a school of thought that was heterogeneous in its expressive modes but had achieved its most intense point of internal unification precisely in the deconstruction of the concept of person.

At its origin, in the early nineteenth century, there was a mixing and mutual influx of the new biological knowledge with philosophical and political thought. The reason why I have given particular attention to this alliance and to the work of the great physiologist Xavier Bichat, in which this mixture began to assume an almost archetypal form, is that – as I will argue throughout the remainder of this book – I am convinced that paradigm shifts (and paradigm leaps to an even greater extent) occur in all the human sciences by incorporating a foreign element, which comes from the lexicon of another discipline. This is the reason for my attempt to trace out the decisive role that linguistics, and then, through it, anthropology, played in the general biologization of politics that has come to be known today as 'biopolitics.' The research devoted by August Schleicher and his successors to the organismic theory of language and to an anthropology which, in its turn, incorporated elements from zoology traces out the contours of an increasingly radical challenge to the modern concept of person as the site of legal imputation and as the rational subject of political action. The theory of a double biological layer within every living being – one vegetative and unconscious, and the other cerebral and relational – was first put forward by Bichat in the form of medical knowledge, then 'translated' by Schopenhauer into philosophical knowledge and by Comte into sociological knowledge. This theorization initiated a process of desubjectivization, which was destined to drastically change the framework of the modern concept of the political. Once human beings were thought to be internally traversed by the tension between two heterogeneous forces and actually determined, in our passions, and even in our will, by a force more in keeping with simple reproductive life, the very premise on which the modern political paradigm was founded could no longer be sustained. If individuals were immersed in the blind corporeality of their vegetative life, incapable even of governing themselves, how could they intentionally create a political order such as to be able to derive their subjective rights from it? If truth be told – this is the conclusion all these thinkers came to, expressed in different ways – not only did the organization of society depend more on a biological given than on the free will of its citizens and on the sovereignty instituted by that will, but this biological given pre-existed both and was inalterable in its overall structure.

When this biopolitical current, which was initially free of any particular ideological connotations, intersected first with the hierarchical anthropology of the late 1800s and then with the emphatically racist anthropology of the early 1900s, the picture quickly changed. The turning point can be identified in the transfer of the dual-life principle from the sphere of the single living being to that of the human species as a whole, which now appeared to be split into two juxtaposed areas of unequal value, and hence endowed with a different right to survival. This is the outcome of a paradigm shift that went beyond a simple lexical contamination between different disciplines. What is registered in this shift is a sort of retroactive effect, or a ricochet perspective, as a result of which the influx of biology into politics was preventively charged with a political significance that was both aggressive and exclusive in nature. The semantic commutator of this genetic mutation in the modern conception, even more than the old linguistic organicism, was an anthroposociology articulated in its turn in terms of comparative zoology. According to this view, humanity was nothing but the infinitely operable set of human types that were differentiated on the basis of how closely or distantly they are related to animal species. Even more than representing the origin of the human species (as Darwin maintained, in a research program that was later co-opted and turned inside out by social Darwinism), the animal thus became a point of division within humanity, between species of people who were separated by their relation to life – and thus to death, since the easy life of some turned out to be directly proportional to the forced death of others. Any idea whatsoever of a formal equality between individuals endowed with a rational will was clearly shattered by this thanatological hold. In the 1930s, the depersonalization project initiated in the previous century from a different perspective reached a point of no return: the notion of person was immediately crushed into its mere biological referent and, rather than philosophically deconstructed, it appeared to be literally devastated.

## 3

But in this case, too, do appearances entirely reflect reality? Without denying the obvious elements of a conflict between the culture of the person and the forms of power/knowledge that have sought to eliminate it at its source, this book adopts a transversal perspective, which makes an entirely affirmative response problematic. When continuities and ruptures are observed from this point of view, rather than appearing in a simple, head-on collision, they arrange themselves in a more complex picture, which defies the linearity of a model based on dichotomy. The idea here is to see double – or rather to displace the phenomena onto two superimposed planes – in a form that does not separate the cracks on the surface from the geological stratum in which they open up. From this perspective, which is of an archaeological or topological slant, what appears to be a negation of principle can take shape as a contrasting complementarity – in other words, as a fold inside the larger figure it is intended to oppose. This different perspectival mode must be applied both to the overt, frontal attack against the category of person, along the line we have just reconstructed, and equally to the response that was mounted in its name at the end of the Second World War. We have seen how Nazism, by fulfilling and at the same time overturning the biopolitical critique of the modern tradition, crushed the person into the individual and the collective body that is its bearer. As demonstrated early on by Emmanuel Levinas,[11] what actually lay at the heart of this deadly project was the elimination from human life of any transcendence with respect to its immediate biological given. No wonder, then, that the great revival of the concept of person, launched on the still smoldering ashes of the Nazi regime, was intended to reopen a gap – a transcendental, if not ontological, difference – between the subject and the biological substrate underlying it. On the other hand, some difference from the body was already implicitly at the core of the notion of person – taken in its original meaning of mask that adheres to the face of the actor, but without being identified with it. The Christian tradition, which soon took possession of the concept, even making it central to the figure of the Trinity, tended to widen that gap by also charging it with a specific metaphysical significance. No matter how inextricably personhood is linked to a living body, the two are not wholly coextensive; and indeed what is most intrinsic to the person, that which allows it to pass into the afterlife, is precisely the fact that it is not coextensive with the body. This defining trait is so fundamental that it recurs, secularized of course, in the

Cartesian dualism between *res extensa* and *res cogitans* and, through it, in modern culture as a whole.

The most enduring trait to be associated with the meaning and fate of the concept of person, however, is that established by Roman law. In this case – especially in this case, actually – the discontinuities, sometimes even radical ones, that mark the internal history of the concept and, to an even greater degree, separate it from the modern legal conception cannot be smoothed over. In no way am I proposing some forward projection of a conceptual apparatus that is tied to its time and thus, clearly, cannot be compared with the subjectivist lexicon that after a certain point left its mark on all subsequent legal history, as has been widely discussed in the literature. Still, there is no denying its subterraneous persistence, like that of some sort of unconscious anachronism that resurfaces at various points in our legal philosophy, setting it at odds with itself. One of these antinomic nodes between the archaic and the contemporary, and by far the most relevant, is what I will from now on refer to as the 'dispositif' of the person, in order to highlight its performative role – I mean a role productive of real effects. It is based on the assumed, continuously recurring separation between person as an artificial entity and the human as a natural being, whom the status of person may or may not befit.[12] This systematic difference is simply the first, the original distinction between abstract categories set up by Roman law, which, in practice, led to some very concrete procedures of exclusion. However, the terrifying constitutive power of this dispositif lies not so much in the normative demarcation it carves out between the different categories as in the zones of indistinguishability it creates at their boundaries – starting with what is, in all senses of the word, the most decisive distinction: the one that characterizes the condition of the slave, situated as he is right in the middle, or in the passage, between person and thing, and thus definable both as a living thing and a reified person.

In reality, the condition of the slave is only the most visible tip of an entire mechanism of social discipline, which works specifically by continuously shifting the categorial thresholds that define, or create, the status of all living beings. Whence the perpetual oscillatory movement between the extremes of person and thing that makes each of them at the same time the opposite and the horizon of the other – not only in the general sense that the definition of the human-as-person emerges negatively out of that of the human-as-thing, but in the more meaningful sense that to experience personhood fully means to keep, or push, other living individuals to the edge of thingness.[13] As I argue in the following pages, this extraordinary performative attitude of Roman legal formalism is particularly recognizable in the two opposite, mirror-image figures of manumission (*manumissio*) and emancipation (*mancipatio*), which, through specific rituals, served to regulate the double cross-flow of personalization and depersonalization. In them, the passage from slavery to freedom and from freedom to slavery, no matter how temporary and reversible, testifies to the always exceptional character of the condition of freedom. Freedom is only an interlude, a sort of unnatural pause on the servile horizon that included within its larger compass all human beings – with the exception of adult male Roman citizens, who themselves only entered into the regime of personhood after a long internship in the entirely subordinate realm of sonship. Whether or not the son's subjection to the power *vitae ac necis* [of giving and taking life] of the *pater* foreshadows a specifically biopolitical type of dominion, one based solely on blood relationship, is still being debated. What is certain, however, is that even in this case – which was generalizable to all citizens of ancient Rome – the process of personification still passed via the status of thingness, where it could very well remain indefinitely.

4

The ancient Roman separation between *homo* and *persona* penetrates like a deep wedge into the philosophical, legal, and political conceptions of the modern era. The reason why this contiguity may not be perceptible to the naked eye is partly that the relations of implication hidden in the semantic upheavals – and even reversals – that run through these conceptions are not easily discernible. Also, the sharp subjectivist turn taken by legal theory, starting at least from the time of natural law, tends to wipe out the footprints of the Roman tradition. In reality, under the thick crust of a strikingly evident lexical transformation, one can glimpse the deeply etched signs of a presence that was never entirely negated by the great jurists. What we are talking about here is not continuity – or, even less, analogy. If anything, the circular figure that this book attempts to retrace is one that unites the opposites at the furthest edge of their contrast: like the points of a circumference, the further away they move from each other, the more they end up joining up again, in the other direction. This is what happened to the idea of person during the epochal transition from the objectivist formalism of Roman law to the individualistic subjectivism of modern rights. The moment these were awarded – at least since the French Revolution, but already by the time of Hobbes – to all humans, who were thus made equal by their common status as subjects, and then as citizens, at that moment the Roman separation between distinct human categories is said to have collapsed, along with the original distance between mask and face: not only because every individual now had its own mask, as it were, but because the mask adhered to the face so intrinsically that it became an integral part of it.

Except that this is not exactly how things went. This story leaves out a fairly major part of reality, which is shown not only by the fact that Hobbes himself separates the person from the body – and does so to the point of making the former the representative of other human, or even non-human, subjects; it is shown by the modern definition itself – the definition of the person, which is now extended, at least in law if not in fact, to all living beings, but only with respect to their moral or rational part. Personhood, it might be said, is that which, in the body, is more than body. Thus the original gap, implicit in the notion that was already formulated by Christian dogma and later reconverted into legal terms, is made to return. In opposition to the biopolitical, and afterwards thanatopolitical line, which tended to unify person and body by crushing the former into the biological matter of the latter, modern personalism, in all its expressions, re-establishes in every individual the separation between personal subject and human being. In this way subjective right, rather than being inherent to the entirety of the human being, applies only to the upper part, which is rational or spiritual in nature, exercising its dominion over the remaining area, which is devoid of these characteristics and therefore thrust into the regime of objecthood. Having rights, from this point of view, really means being subjected to one's own objectification. This is precisely the definition of the person proposed by Jacques Maritain while he was actively engaged in drafting the Universal Declaration of 1948: person-hood is qualified as the sovereignty that each human being exercises over his or her animal being. The contrastive symmetry with the two lives that Bichat talked about is hard to ignore, even though the relation of dominance between them is clearly inverted: Bichat assigns it to the vegetative and irrational part, while Maritain assigns it to the rational and voluntary part. What remains common, however, is the placement, inside the human being, of a non-human aspect, which in the first case is destined to overcome us and in the second to be mastered by us. Whether you choose to view the philosophy of the person as an unconscious (or even denied) form of biopolitics, or anti-personalist biopolitics as an inner fold of the dispositif of the person, either way we are defined by our relationship with the animal that both dwells inside us and alters us. At the root of this convergence lies, of course, the Aristotelian definition of the human being as a rational animal, adopted in the first case from the point of view of our animality and, in the second, from that of our rationality. Because of this shared assumption, contrary to first appearances perhaps, biopolitical corporealization of the person and spiritualistic personalization of the body are inscribed inside the same theoretical circle.

The avenue for breaking open this circle lies in a comprehensive revision of the relations of contiguity and opposition established by the interpretive tradition. We have talked about the relationship between ancient Roman law and the modern legal conception of the person. Something similar has to be said about the relationship between biopolitics and liberalism, one that is oppositional only in appearance. It might even be posited that liberalism is in fact the antinomic juncture between the ancient – and recent – philosophy of the person and its opposing school, reproducing its assumptions in an inverted form. In question, once again, is the differentiating nexus between person and body. For the liberal view, as represented by Locke or Mill, the body is owned by the person who dwells inside it. This aspect alone underscores the radical distance and fundamental difference of liberalism from Nazi biocracy: while the latter works on the human species as a whole, the former pertains only to the individual. Moreover, while Nazism assigned ownership of the body to state sovereignty, the liberal conception assigned ownership to the person implanted inside the body. But this basic heterogeneity also provides a measure of the trait of symmetry, defined, for both, by a productivist view of life – a life made to serve in one case the superior destiny of the chosen race and, in the other, the maximum expansion of individual freedom. Only that this freedom comes by way of a potential reduction of the body to an appropriated thing. The point of suture between these opposites is always relative to the definition of person. To be the owner of a body, the person cannot be coextensive with it; in fact, the person is specifically defined by the distance that separates it from the body. If you look at the bioethics developed as part of the liberal tradition, you find, in its ultimate form, the ancient Roman separation between *persona* and *homo*: both for Hugo Engelhardt and for Peter Singer, while not all human beings are persons, neither are all persons human beings. Hence the resulting gradation – or degradation – from full person to semi-person, non-person, and anti-person, represented respectively by the adult, the infant or disabled adult, the incurably ill, and the insane. Hence to each level of personalization – or depersonalization – there corresponds a different right to determination, and even preservation of one's life. Here, too, in formulations that closely recall the sovereign power of the *paterfamilias* over his children and over anyone whose condition is a reified reproduction of that state, the personhood-deciding machine marks the final difference between what must live and what can be legitimately cast to death.

## 5

As far-reaching and widespread as the logic of the person is in its genealogy and effects, it does not occupy the entire contemporary horizon. Opposed to it, in ways that are not always recognizable and sometimes are only barely sketched out, is thought on the impersonal. The third chapter of this book examines some of its figures, or segments, drawn mainly from twentieth-century philosophy. I could have chosen other references – from contemporary art, especially from painting, music and film, which have long aimed at a deconstruction of the personal subject.[14] I have preferred to focus on philosophy for this discussion in order to provide a preliminary theoretical grid for an object that is elusive practically by definition, precisely because it has always been emarginated, or overwhelmed, by the various forms of power/ knowledge of the person. Which is why this part of my inquiry cannot be developed in a linear or coherent fashion. Its heterogeneity, even fragmentariness, is structural, not contingent; in the sense that, rather than having to do with the tonal diversity of the texts and authors involved, it relates to the negative nature of a category that takes on meaning only through contrast with another category, which is assumed to be prior to it or superimposed on it. Some immediate clarification needs to be provided about this as well. Of course the impersonal lies outside the horizon of the person, but not in a place that is unrelated to it: the impersonal is situated, rather, at the confines of the personal; on the lines of resistance, to be exact, which cut through its territory, thus preventing, or at least opposing, the functioning of its exclusionary dispositif. The impersonal is a shifting border: that critical margin, one might say, that separates the semantics of the person from its natural effect of separation; that blocks its reifying outcome. The impersonal does not negate the personal frontally, as a philosophy of the anti-person would; rather, the impersonal is its alteration, or its extroversion into an exteriority that calls it into question and overturns its prevailing meaning.

This complex – rather than merely oppositional – relation of the impersonal to the person is what explains the 'third' figure that lends its name to this entire inquiry. Rather than destroying the person – as the thanatopolitics of the twentieth century claimed to do, although it ended up reinforcing it instead – to do conceptual work on the 'third person' means creating an opening to a set of forces that push it beyond its logical, and even grammatical boundaries. This strategy of estrangement or outflanking responds perfectly to what is effectively the founding text: Émile Benveniste's study of personal pronouns, which opens the third chapter. If there is anything that surpasses its natural relevance to linguistic issues, something invested with so much meaning that it illuminates the entire set of questions raised, it is Benveniste's insistence on the difference of the third person, in both its pronominal and verbal forms, from the first and second person. Unlike them, it is the only one that does not have personal connotations, to the point where it can be defined as a 'non-person': not only because it refers to something or someone that cannot be circumscribed within a specific subject – in the sense that it can relate to everyone and no one – but, more profoundly, because it completely evades the dialogical regime of interlocution inside of which the other two remain fixed. This absolute specificity (the third person is the only one to be both singular and plural) stands out all the more in the unbreakable, even specular, connection that binds the first person to the second: in the discursive context, whether implicitly or explicitly, the *I* always addresses a *you*, just as a *you* always pre-supposes an *I* that designates it as such, before being substituted to it in the role of subject of the utterance. This is a necessity, one that reveals the rhetorical character of all philosophies of the second person (from Martin Buber to Vladimir Jankélévitch and beyond), whose logics always remain within the status of the first person, despite their claims of surpassing it. In fact, regardless of the mode of relationship said to exist between the two – direct or reversed, frontal or oblique, horizontal or vertical – the *you* only takes on meaning from the *I* that interpellates it, whether in the form of a command, an invocation, or a prayer. The 'two' is nec-essarily inscribed in the logic of the 'one,' just as 'one' always tends to split into 'two' in order to be able to mirror and recognize itself in its human or divine interlocutor.

## 6

But, once this essential difference between the third person and the others has been established, the question arises as to how it is figured in the various philosophies of the impersonal. Firstly, it is figured as justice, understood in a form that is opposed both to the objective law of Roman origin and to the subjective law of the modern sort. This radical option lies at the heart of Simone Weil's thought. The direct line that Weil, in opposition to the personalist tradition of Maritain, draws between the privative, exclusive char-acter of the law and the generalization of the idea of person casts a bright beam of light onto the scene we are exploring. To counter the nihilistic effects of this connection, one that seems to stretch like a sinister shadow all the way from Rome to the Nazi regime, Weil asserts the truth of the impersonal with unprecedented clarity. What is sacred in humans is not their *persona*; it is that which is not covered by their mask. Only this has a chance of reforging the relationship between humanity and rights that was interrupted by the immunitary machine of the person, and of making possible something as seemingly contradictory as a 'a common right' or a 'right in common.' Everyone, from Alexandre Kojève and Vladimir Jankélévitch to Emmanuel Levinas, who insists on the essential – rather than simply functional – impartiality or neutrality of the law, on its condition of being a third party with respect to prosecution and defense, merely repeats from differing points of view the need first articulated by Weil. In each of them, the third person is what hails the advent of a law that can finally be translated into justice. If, for Kojève, this lies at the end of history, when human beings will reimmerse themselves in their animal nature, Jankélévitch both affirms and denies this fact, by placing it after the face-to-face relationship of love. Situated between the two thinkers, Levinas traces out a more complex position, attempting to reconcile the exclusive responsibility of the relationship between two persons with the requirement for universal justice toward the third by making them overlap.

That this attempt is destined to fail precisely because of the irreducibility of a ternary logic to a binary one is just a symptom of a deeper contradiction, which can be traced to the very nature of the third person. We have already remarked on the fact that the third person is not actually another person – with respect to the first and second – but rather something that extends out of the logic of the person, in favor of a different regime of meaning. When Maurice Blanchot identifies the third person with the enigmatic figure of the neuter, or neutral, he is seeking to remove it, preventively, from any undue personalization. The neuter is not another person to be added to the first two, but rather what is *neither* one *nor* the other and what defies all dichotomies founded on, or presupposed by, the language of the person. For this reason it is not located at any particular point in the interlocutory relation – high or low, at the center, or on the side, as Levinas would have it – but most definitely outside interlocution, so much so that it ends up being identical with the placeless space of the 'outside.' From this radical breach of the dialogical model adopted by all the philosophies of the first and second person stems an attitude manifested in the entire philosophical tradition: the misunderstanding of – or open hostility toward – a figure like that of the neuter, which is persistently negated or tamed in all its disruptive effects. The only force able to stand up to it, says Blanchot, is writing. In writing – where talk *of* the neutral gives place to talking *in* the neutral or giving voice *to* the neutral – neither the author nor the character has the chance of saying 'I' (and therefore 'you'); thus they inscribe themselves in the impersonal regime of 'one' ['*si*']. Instead of a subject of an action, what comes out of this is an action with no subject, or an action that coincides with the subject in the non-predictability of the event. Blanchot's erasure of his name from collective documents written between the 1960s and the 1970s was an attempt, albeit a highly problematic one, to transfer the experience of the impersonal from the world of literature to the world of politics: in other words, to do politics in the third person.

How? How does one go about making the impersonal not only a power for deconstructing the ancient – and new – dispositif of the person, but also the form, or, better still, the content of a practice that alters existence? How are we to introduce that ulteriority, or that exteriority, into our individual and collective experience? This is the first and last question to receive attention from both Michel Foucault and Gilles Deleuze, at a tangential point of focus that went far beyond mere friendship, because it touched on something not specifically related to persons, but to the preindividual or transindividual domain that precedes and traverses them. For both, the figurative form assumed by the third person is life; but the routes they take to get there are very different. Foucault, like Blanchot, passes via the outside – along that 'oceanic line' which skirts the abyss of death while resisting it. As Bichat had done in his own way, Foucault also takes death and its utter estrangement as his starting point to arrive at life. He proceeds by pushing the outside further and further outside, externalizing what is already external, until it is transformed into its opposite: what is more external than the external, if not an inside more internal than any interiority? The outside appears so elusive to us precisely because it is inside us – we view ourselves from a perspective that does not fit with the perspective of personal subjectivity, and indeed clashes with it. Life, one might say, is a biological stratum that, for Foucault, is never coextensive with subjectivity because it is always caught in a dual, simultaneous process of subjection and subjectification: it is the space that power lays siege to without ever managing to occupy it fully, even generating continuously new forms of resistance. From this perspective we can make out the still hazy outlines of an affirmative biopolitics, one that is not defined negatively with respect to the dispositifs of modern power/ knowledge but is rather situated along the line of tension that traverses and displaces them.

Although oriented toward the same outcome, the direction Deleuze takes is different. It proceeds through folding rather than exteriorization. The issue at stake is still the question of imma-nence, but he does not arrive at it negatively, as Foucault does, through the transcendence of transcendance or the externalization of the external. For Deleuze, immanence is not generated dialecti-cally by transcendence, as in Hegel, nor is it traversed by tran-scendence, as in the phenomenological or in the Heideggerian tradition. Immanence is nothing but the fold of being onto itself, its declension into becoming. This is what life is – it is always *a* life: not that which resists death, arising out of this struggle, but rather that which separates death from itself, unfolding it in a continuous process of change. Hence the deconstruction of the person in all its expressions – theological, legal, and philosophical. What fades away from the plane of immanence is precisely that difference based on personhood that has always located the subject outside the corporeal substrate inside of which it is implanted, just as substance has always been separated from its modes. This does not mean – even in Deleuze, especially not in Deleuze – making what we call the subject the inert, passive receptor of the event. On the contrary: identifying the subject with the event means endowing the subject with the ability to 'counter-actualize' it – that is, to fold it in a different, or even opposite direction from the initial one. It means to choose, *in* the event, the most unex-pected inclination, the one that is least blocked up in its presup-posed determination. It is difficult for a tradition like ours, soaked to its roots in political theology, to sever the category of decision from its connection with the categories of the individual and of sovereignty, to ally it with the impersonal instead of the personal. But this is precisely what Deleuze does – through a theory of virtuality which, by breaking with the metaphysical alternative (or coextension) of the possible and necessary, opens identity up to the multiple play of differences. The extreme, almost posthumous figure of 'becoming-animal,' which seems to bring in the present, by anticipation, the prehuman or posthuman image that Kojève had envisaged for the end of history, opens thought on the impersonal onto a perspective whose significance as a whole remains to be understood. What takes form from this perspective, now standing outside the fateful silhouette of the person (and thus also of the thing), is more than freedom from the fundamental interdiction of our time. It is also our signpost for the reuniting of form and force, mode and substance, *bios* and *zoe* – which has always been promised but never truly experienced until now.

# 1

# The Double Life
## The Machine of the Human Sciences

---

### 1

In the early 1800s, the concept of person – understood as a rational subject capable of self-determination in relationship with other individuals endowed with the same characteristics – was rocked by a crisis originating outside of political theory, in the field of biology. As often happens in times of paradigm shift, the impact that was crucial in creating the effects of change came from outside the discipline. Our modern political categories, for that matter, now in dispute, came into being marked by contamination with secularized theological concepts. There is a difference, however: what entered into the legal–political vocabulary then was a transcendental element; now we are talking about a material, or a substance, like life, which is immanent. What is even more symptomatic of the dialectic that occurs between the various sciences of man is that this concept of life, destined to profoundly change the political lexicon, itself had political connotations. From its earliest formulations, the notion of life investigated by the new biological knowledge was specifically defined by its absolute conflict with death. The best way to grasp the extraordinary novelty of Xavier Bichat's work – and the reason why it met with such popularity in the first half of the nineteenth century, even by comparison to the vitalist view it is usually associated with – is by focusing on the threatening presence of death that looms over life from both inside and outside it. The classic vitalists, like Bordeu or Barthez, limited themselves to removing the living organism from the general laws of physics, and by doing so they ended up depriving it of a normative principle capable of unifying its variety of expressions within a scientifically described framework. Bichat, on the other hand, identified the specific status of the living body precisely in its active opposition to the pressure of death. When he writes, in the famous opening words of his *Recherches*, that "life is the totality of those functions which resist death,"[1] we are meant to take this statement in the sense of a conflict without truce. In the body, life and death confront each other as opposing powers whose tendency is to outdo each other in a zero-sum game in which the advancement of one means the retreat, or breakdown, of the other: "The measure of life then, in general, is the difference which exists between the effort of external powers, and of internal resistance. The excess of the former announces its weakness; the predominance of the latter is an indication of its strength."[2]

It would be difficult to find traces of a more intensely political lexicon in biological knowledge than the one adopted by Bichat at the dawn of modern physiology. As Georges Canguilhem points out, its metaphors are based on the art of war:[3] action–reaction, attack–defense, and power–resistance are among the most commonly used words in a story whose topic is the survival or the extermination of *bios*. A definition of life can seemingly be conceived only within a semantic orbit marked by the necessity for deadly conflict: to the death and with death. The first part of the book, dedicated to a general definition of life, only takes on meaning and consistency in association with the second, which is devoted to a detailed phenomenology of the various types of death. The fact that Bichet (who died at the age of 31) during his short life opened up and examined thousands of corpses of people who had come to a violent death – people who, for the most part, were guillotined during the Terror – has a deeper significance, perhaps, than that of a mere biographical curiosity. "What is observation worth if we are ignorant of the seat of disease [*mal*]? Open a few bodies, this obscurity will soon disappear, which observation alone would never have been able to have dissipated."[4]

More than a clinical suggestion, this famous proposition from the *Anatomie générale* sounds like a grand curtain sweeping the scene open onto the constitutive interweaving between death and knowledge of life. To arrive at the deepest truth about a body, medical science is forced to insinuate itself into the same cut that etched death into the body, and then redouble it. As Michel Foucault expressed it, only the clear light of death can illuminate, like a lightning flash, the dark night of life, revealing the logical and epistemological predominance of death over life.[5] This predominance is exercised primarily from the outside, by the environmental forces that squeeze life into a circle it cannot break and whose fatal power it can only resist as long as its own energy remains. But then, at the same time, death also exercises its ascendancy from inside the body, where its possibility, indeed its necessity, takes seat from the moment of birth, like a tumor that grows progressively and inexorably. Rather than a clean cut that chops off the head in a single sweep, death appears as a dull murmur accompanying and silently gnawing at every moment of life, distributing itself into many little deaths, which only at a certain point join together to form one lethal event.

Into this framework of partial deaths, local entropies and continuous, unbridled mortality is also introduced the phenomenon of apparent death: a posthumous survival in which death seems to hang back and retreat before the unexpected return of life. What is its basis? What other truth does this enigmatic and disturbing phenomenon give voice to? Bichat's answer, in many ways decisive, is that this duplication of death points to a duplication of life itself. Apparent death – death that is not absolute and in which an interval occurs between its first appearance on the scene and its final victory – is the reversed expression of the preliminary gap between life's two modes of being. Or rather, between the two lives that make up all life: organic life, to which Bichat ascribes the vegetative functions (digestion, respiration, circulation of the blood) and animal life, which governs the motor, sensory, and intellectual activities involving relations with the outside. While organic life is closed and inward-looking, animal life is in contact with the environment, changing it and being changed by it. While no principle of symmetry is to be found in organic life – there is one heart, one stomach, one liver – animal life is organized in a symmetrical and binary fashion, as is clear from the correspondence of the eyes, ears, and arms. But the aspect that appears to capture Bichat's attention even more, just as we saw in the relationship of death to life, is the functional and quantitative prevalence of organic life over animal life. First, in the sense that organic life continues even during sleep, while animal life is instead interrupted, resuming only when the organism wakes up again. But also, and even more, in the sense that there is organic life before birth, when the fetus experiences only a nutritive life, and at the end, with the advent of death, when organic life continues for some time after animal life has ended, as can be seen from the growth of nails and hair even after the 'first' death. A double death, in short, is matched by a double life, which has unequal importance not only because it is geared for different purposes, but also because it has a different intensity.[6]

Without stopping to look in greater detail at the clinical consequences of this difference – one that is crucial in deciding, for example, on the possibility of transplanting organs that are still alive after brain death – what really matters for our inquiry is the transversal consequence it leads to in other discourses, especially in the lexicon of political philosophy. This explains why this difference is constantly picked up by writers and texts not directly concerned with physiological research but, precisely for this reason, expressive of the significance that the life sciences have in shaping philosophy and politics. The question that gets entangled here first and foremost is the relationship between the nature of the living subject and the form of political action. This is where the disruptive effects of Bichat's model are discharged: at this point of tangency where the categories intersect. While, as we know, the unquestioned assumption of modern political philosophy is that of subjects endowed with a rational will who, by collective choice, establish a certain political order, the physiological principle of a 'double life,' naturally in a form external to the intentions of its author, creates a significant shift in perspective. If we take the position of Hobbes as a reference point, the criterion of the founding break between the natural state and the political state is called into question, as is the logical path that leads to the covenant, and thus to the establishment of order. Not only because life can never break its biological link with nature, but because life itself is 'decided' ['*decisa*'], or cut off[7] from a distinction prior to any other decision and destined to weigh heavily on it. If the passions, for example – which Hobbes had placed at the origin of the civil choice – derive from organic life and not from animal life, as Bichat clearly claims, no acts based on them can any longer be attributed to rational motivations. Not only that, but, strictly speaking, a political subject does not even exist as a source of voluntary action, because the will, although linked to animal life, is deeply innervated in a bodily system that is sustained and to a large extent governed by its vegetative part. This alone – far beyond the intentions of Bichat, as we said earlier – opens up an avenue, by itself disruptive to modern conceptual language, which leads toward a radical desubjectivization of human praxis. What begins to break down, or at least become unrecognizable in its canonical formulation, is the very idea of the person, understood as a site of legal and political imputation. With its classic prerogatives already under attack from the overwhelming pressure of death, the person now appears further decentralized by being split into two overlapping – or underlapping – zones that preclude any unified image for it. Divided into a 'life inside' and a 'life outside,' into a vegetal life and an animal life, the person is traversed by a power that is foreign to it, which shapes its instincts, emotions, and desires into a form that can no longer be ascribed to a single element. It is as if a non-human – something different from and earlier than animal nature itself – had taken up residence in the human being; or as if it had always been there, with dissolutive effects on the personal modality of this being. From this moment on, the role of politics – now inevitably biopolitics – will no longer be to define the relationship between human beings as much as to identify the precise point at which the frontier is located between what is human and what, inside the human itself, is other than human.

2

The deconstruction of the subject that Bichat carried out in the world of biology had a profound effect on philosophy, most notably on the work of Schopenhauer. True, other thinkers starting with Hegel had explicitly referred to the author of the *Recherches*. But, for them, Bichat remained an external relation. For Schopenhauer, the relation became so entirely intrinsic that it took the form of an out-and-out identification with "this distinguished man who was snatched from the world at so early an age," the author of "one of the most profoundly conceived works in the whole of French literature."[8] The opposition between organic life and animal life, which Schopenhauer ascribes to his own opposition between will and intellect, lies at the heart of this identification. If Bichat seems to ascribe the will to animal life, this must not be misinterpreted, says Schopenhauer, cautioning the reader against an insufficiently radical reading of the *Recherches*. What Bichat is speaking about, he explains, is conscious free choice: deliberation and estimation of the motives, whose product appears as an act of will; not true desire, which is blind and opaque and exclusively ascribable to organic life. Once this switch in terminology is made clear, Schopenhauer is convinced that their work corresponds perfectly: "His reflections and mine mutually support each other, since his are the physiological commentary on mine, and mine the philosophical commentary on his; and we shall best be understood by being read side by side."[9] There are essentially two topical *loci* in this full-blown convergence, and they are interconnected within a single discursive frame. First, the passions are part of the vegetative life, the same one that the sphere of the will belongs to. Second, as a consequence, the moral character is immutable: since it is rooted in the organic layer of the living being, it cannot be altered by education or by the external environment. The conclusion that Schopenhauer draws from this is a forceful rejection of the Cartesian thesis – relaunched not long before, first by Franz Joseph Gall and later by Jean-Marie Pierre Flourens – according to which acts of will are equivalent to thoughts. The unity of life – in full harmony with the perspective opened up by Bichat – is no longer broken down by the old dualism between body and soul, but by the biological difference between an organic type of "life within" and a relational "life outside."

It would be hard to imagine a more violent blow to the consciousness-based tradition of modern thought. It strikes at that inseparable nucleus of will and reason, tearing apart the quintessence of what a whole line of thought defined as the subject (or the person), taking as its point of departure precisely the distance of this subject from – or at least its non-coincidence with – the body inside of which it is in any case lodged. Not that Schopenhauer opposes the sphere of the will to that of the body: on the contrary, he makes them overlap in a narrow metaphysics that construes one as the objectification of the another. The philosophical consequences of this shift are well known. What concerns us most deeply, however, is the political (or rather, at this point, decidedly biopolitical) effects that they entail. A comparison with Hobbes's position is, as usual, illuminating as to the real paradigm shift signaled in this move. Schopenhauer is far from rejecting the anthropological aspect, so to speak, of the Hobbesian device – leading the natural state back to the *bellum omnium contra omnes*. If anything, he takes it to even more extreme conclusions. Nature, itself an expression of the unstoppable will to live that governs the world, is traversed, and indeed even constituted, by a relentless struggle between all its components. This starts at the level of inorganic crystals and moves up, to the vegetal kingdom and then to the animal kingdom, where the conflict is so destructive that it turns its violence against whoever makes the first move, in a sort of perpetual self-devouring:

> The young hydra, which grows like a bud out of the old one, and afterwards separates itself from it, fights while it is still joined to the old one for the prey that offers itself, so that the one snatches it out of the mouth of the other. But the bulldog-ant of Australia affords us the most extraordinary example of this kind; for if it is cut in two, a battle begins between the head and tail. The head seizes the tail with its teeth, and the tail defends itself bravely by stinging the head: the battle may last for half an hour, until they die or are dragged away by other ants.[10]

The reason for this fighting to death – or more properly, to a double death, first of the whole and then of the individual pieces – is mainly the infinitely expansive nature of the desire for life that is woven into the fabric of the individual, who is led to see every other individual as a simple product of his or her own representation, and thus disposable at will.[11] But then, more profoundly, the reason lies in the fact that those individual differences are only the external refraction, the multiplied image of a single will, and therefore a will that is permanently in conflict with itself due to its irrepressible vital impulse. This is why there is no real remedy for interhuman conflict. At most, conflict may be limited or restricted to forms destined sooner or later to be overwhelmed by the deadly force that traverses and rouses them once again. Every success, every victory of the higher forces, which are designed to feed on the lower ones, carries in itself the resistance of these lower forms. Like a worm, it weakens them, gradually sucking them into their emptiness, until they are claimed by death, which had stalked them from the beginning:

> Hence also in general the burden of physical life, the necessity of sleep, and, finally, of death; for at last these subdued forces of nature, assisted by circumstances, win back from the organism, wearied even by the constant victory, the matter it took from them, and attain to an unimpeded expression of their being [...] This seems to have been running in the mind of Jacob Böhm when he says somewhere that all the bodies of men and animals, and even all plants, are really half dead.[12]

Just as Bichat viewed death as arriving from both outside and inside life, for Schophenhauer, too, when life attempts to escape death's dominion, it reaches out and pulls life back. As in the living being – whether animal or human, now distinguished only by a difference of degree rather than of essence – the lower, organic part quantitatively dominates the upper, cerebral part, determining, or at least influencing it in all its forms. Similarly, even though death makes life possible through the conflict between individuals and through the succession of generations, it will always prevail over life. This cyclical, natural mechanism in which the individual is nothing but an instrument for the expansion of the species cannot be stopped by any artificial or technical contrivance. Hence the full resumption of Hobbes's negative anthropology in Schopenhauer is matched by a forceful rejection of the Hobbesian political solution. Not because Schopenhauer rejects the idea of covenant in principle (he refers to it at least formally), but because this idea is emptied of meaning, as a consequence of the impossibility of passing from the natural to the civil state. Although this transition was possible, and indeed necessary in the modern notion of subjectivity – defined precisely by the primacy of the rational will over a separate body dominated by it – the passage is literally unthinkable for human beings who are not only crushed into their bodies, but also largely governed by its vegetative part. In this case, obviously, there can be no passage such as the one that occurs in Hobbes, from fear, innervated throughout the organic component along with the other passions, to any form of political rationality.

This is the origin of an explicitly negative concept of the law – one derived, in other words, not from the need for affirmative justice but rather for its opposite: "According to this, the concept of wrong is the original and positive, and the concept of right, which is opposed to it, is the derivative and negative."[13] Right, ungraspable in itself, is nothing but the negative or the destructive, namely the will to live. It is clear that in this radically biopolitical horizon, the state, which is certainly needed to impose order, cannot enjoy any of the moral attributes still conferred on it by Hegel. Far from being ethical, or a bearer of freedom, it derives from the same egotism that it must control through harsh coercion – not by eliminating conflict, since it is inevitable, but merely by transferring it from the inside to the outside: from conflict within the state to war between states. This is why the state device is far from achieving a peaceful outcome. Primarily, because this goal is unattainable in itself. But also because, even if it were attainable, it would lead to a consequence – an excess of life – that would be intolerable for those who live in, and thanks to, the space opened up by death's work: "And even supposing that all this were finally overcome and removed, by wisdom founded on the experience of thousands of years, at the end the result would be the actual over-population of the whole planet," concludes Schopenhauer, "the terrible evil of which only a bold imagination can now realise."[14]

## 3

Up until this moment, the influence of biological knowledge on political thought had been objective and unintended, so to speak;

but the time came when this influence was received and established on a theoretical plane as well. This change in perception had its source in the work of Auguste Comte, which strikes us as archaic only because it is basically extraneous to the backbone of modernity. With the coining of the term "biocracy" in the introduction to his *Système de politique positive*,[15] a term preparatory to the later "sociocracy," one may well say that a conceptual vocabulary outside the semantics of democracy was established. Henceforth, *demos* – all parties united in a common national identity – was no longer the horizon of reference for power; rather that horizon was *bios*, the life of an organism, whether individual or collective, now external to and exceeding any conventional legal or political formulation.

It should come as no surprise that, at the source of this categorical shift, albeit issuing from a more fluid and varied assessment, there appears the name of "the incomparable Bichat,"[16] to whose "profound insight" we owe not only the transfer of the "first rank among the natural sciences from Astronomy to Biology,"[17] but also the crucial difference between animal functions and vegetal functions that defines the relationship between "life within" and "life outside." This point, however, is exactly what prompts the critique undertaken by Comte, which is relevant to subsequent biopolitical formulations. Unlike Bichat, who interpreted the relationship between life and environment in terms of a living organism's resistance to the powers of death coming from the outside, Comte leads it to a more complex dialectic: if everything surrounding living bodies really tended to destroy them, their conditions of existence would fail to hold up. But this is not the case. Only when the environment undergoes radical perturbations does its influence become destructive; otherwise it tends to preserve a life that can interact with it in its turn.[18] Now this reference to 'conditions of existence,' garnered primarily from Henri de Blainville (in addition to Georges Couvier), is doubly significant. Not only because it lays out a more sophisticated scheme than the rigidly bipolar one established by Bichat (living nature versus lifeless nature), but also because, in reality, it affects the relation of predominance established by him between organic life and animal life in the human being. Not that Comte disputes the importance of the vegetative part that links humans to all other living beings; but he locates the specificity of the human in the possibility, albeit partial and problematic, of overturning this primacy in favor of animal life. Although always driven by a natural, biological impulse, in certain circumstances humans can come to break the cycle of individual self-preservation for the purpose of social order.

This is the always reversible passage from the level of "biocracy" to that of "sociocracy." There is a biunivocal relation between the two spheres: just as the first constitutes the necessary root of the second, so the second is intended to act systematically in response to the first. The same relation of implication and reversibility connects biology with politics, as well as with all the other sciences laid out in Comte's encyclopedia. If, through the taxonomic principle, biology becomes the model for the other disciplines, and especially for political science and sociology, the latter reinterpret the taxonomic classification in a hierarchical key, which is reflected in turn in the biological process. The basic premise that governs the whole machinery of the human sciences is the need for any disciplinary language to be able to progress and gain complexity only by going beyond its original boundaries, in order to seek outside itself tools that are able to validate their own epistemic status. Following this line of reasoning, knowledge of life is, for Comte, the exteriority inside of which political science, even before seeking answers, must seek the questions that cannot be framed in its own vocabulary. From Montesquieu to Condorcet, not to mention Rousseau, the mistake of modern political philosophy is that it failed to understand this necessity. Although these thinkers started out on the right path, by bringing political phenomena back to invariable laws of nature, at some point all of them lost contact with a general knowledge of life, falling back on abstract and doctrinal principles, which caused them to stray from reality. Not only that, in trying to break free from metaphysical absolutism, says Comte, they ushered into play concepts such as natural law, sovereignty, general will, which, albeit secularized, are themselves in some ways tributaries of a theological–political horizon. Hence the need for his new positive philosophy, a radical deconstruction not only of democratic theory, but also of the entire political–legal structure in which it has its roots:

The word *Right* should be excluded from political language, as the word *Cause* from the language of philosophy. Both are theological and metaphysical conceptions; and the former is as immoral and subversive as the latter is unmeaning and sophistical. Both are alike incompatible with the final state; and their value during the revolutionary period of modern history has simply consisted in their solvent action upon previous systems. Rights, in the strict sense of the word, are possible only so long as power is considered as emanating from a superhuman will.[19]

What thus emerges is a further boost to the process of desubjectivization, or depersonalization, whose beginnings we reconstructed in the previous pages. What led to the results of the revolutionary years, both anarchic and despotic in character as they were, was the Enlightenment's idea that the organization of society could depend on the free will of individuals or on legal principles arising from the mind of a legislator. In reality, both the free will of individuals and the legal principles are themselves the historical and natural results of an already given order, which people can (and certainly must) improve, but not overturn in an arbitrary manner. In short, the subject cannot create the world anew – as the secularized theology of modern revolutions, but also the democratic logic of the sovereign people, would like – because the subject is a part of the world, located inside it. But – and this is the crucial point – for the subject, being inside the world means to be somehow outside oneself, to be part of something that at the same time includes and transcends oneself. This something is life: not only of the single individual but of the large collective body that includes the individual, while exceeding it, in the totality of humankind.[20]

When Comte argues that in sociology "it would now be considered a serious heresy, equally repugnant to good sense and to morality, to define Humanity by Man, instead of referring Man to Humanity,"[21] what he means is that the subject, as conceived of from Descartes on, only acquires a body when it is reconceived in the biological form of life. But he also intends us to understand that human life realizes itself by looking out onto what lies outside it, at the border with its environmental otherness, where its origin and its destiny become recognizable. Already the idea that the human species is not alone in the world, but rather shares a large part of its nature with other living beings who are contiguous to it, creates a breach in the anthropocentric prejudice of man's absolute superiority: "It is a very irrational disdain" writes Comte "which makes us object to all comparison between human society and the social state of the lower animals. This unphilosophical pride arose out of the protracted influence of the theologico-metaphysical philosophy."[22] It is this relationship with the animal that protects Comte's critique of democratic egalitarianism from any aristocratic, or even racist slant, in contrast to "the insolent pride which induces some ranks of society to suppose themselves as, in a manner, of another species than the rest of mankind."[23] But, for Comte, the most decisive vehicle for decentering the person-subject is the concept of death, inseparable from that of life. The shocking growth in the number of deaths in the great body of humanity, as it has developed over the course of history, does not constitute an offence to life – something it must defend itself against and resist, as Bichat would still have it – but rather it is what simultaneously allows life both continuation and change. Just as one generation succeeds the previous one, as the newly born take the place of others – those from whom they came – similarly, those who die open up a space to live in for those who will replace them. Inevitably embedded in life, death constitutes both its absolute outside and the internal center of irradiation from which living beings experience the limits of their own identity and the extent of their alteration.

4

As long as we remain within the horizon traced out by the founding role of biology in relation to the other disciplines of knowledge – political theory in particular – the classical notion of person (together with the associated notions of individual rights and state sovereignty) begins to show cracks in its underlying assumptions but has yet to be frontally negated. Comte's sociocracy, with its methodological openings and anti-modern tendencies, represents a fragile balance in this dialectic. The real break that led toward a different logic, one that was intensively biopolitical rather than simply biophilosophical, required a new passage created by the productive intersection with the vocabulary of anthropology. The biologistic reformulation of modern political philosophy took on a normative significance destined to transform it radically, in a direction that was prescriptive and exclusionary. This happened not by abandoning the key categories of the previous perspective, but by subjecting them to a different conceptual register that, on its own, altered and distorted their effect. This is exactly what happened to the fundamental binary division made by Bichat, transferred from individual physiology – the individual body of each person – to the human species taken as a whole and in its development. In this shift in scale, anthropological discourse, which was politicized in its turn by hierarchical leanings, fulfilled its strategic role as a semantic commutator: what in Bichat's formulation was a functional difference of a purely biological character now acquired the meaning of a comparative decision based on different levels of humanity.

To grasp the scope of this general shift in categories that arose from anthropological knowledge in mid-nineteenth century, we need to go back to a text published in 1837 by Victor Courtet de l'Isle under the programmatic title *Political Science Founded on the Science of Man or Study of Human Races*. The author starts from the preliminary observation that the human, like any other living being, can be analyzed as an individual or as a member of a given species, genus, or race. While the first type of study concerns the physiological or psychological sciences, depending on whether the focus is placed on the subject's physical or moral aspect, the second makes up the specific territory of anthropology. Now the basic thesis of Courtet is that the constitutive weakness of modern political thought stems from the fact that, first, it has focused on the individual rather than on the species; and, second, it has focused on the psychological rather than the physiological. What is more, what was defined as political science – for example by Montesquieu – believed itself capable of deriving the characteristics of the various regimes or systems of government from external factors, such as climate, education, and customs, thereby ignoring the most intrinsic, and thus most crucial, factor: the natural–biological difference that separates the various human groups from each other. What matters in actual political life is not what springs from the subjective and voluntary choices of individuals, but what precedes and determines them, from within their specific nature, with the peremptory necessity of an originary mold:

> Man is not only an instrument, he is also endowed with an active, intrinsic power. Thus we should not limit ourselves to solely analyzing the influences that man is subject to: we must also analyze the influence of his faculties, his native predispositions. Now, let us state the truth: man differs in his faculties and native predispositions on the basis of the *race* to which he belongs, in other words on the basis of differences in organization resulting from the plurality of races.[24]

It is true, he admits, that for some time now (an explicit reference to Gall's phrenology, but one that may well extend to Bichat's physiology) political science has been receptive to the contributions of biology, identifying the source of a given thought in a certain fold of the brain, or deriving a character-based attitude from the shape of the skull. But this approach, although productive and indispensable today to criminal pathology, for example, has been kept within the confines of individual analysis and not extended to the study of populations as distinct ethnic assemblages, which is the specific object of political knowledge. The comparative anthropology of races responds precisely to this need. Far from presupposing the unity of the human species, comparative anthropology is the rigorous science of its internal differences, which, as such, because they are rooted in the deepest stratum of our nature, are insuperable. Only by delving deeper, by penetrating inside, can the constitutive relation between life and politics avoid the abstractness of philosophical musings and the arbitrariness of psychological introspection in order to tap into a more concrete level of collective life. On the basis of these assumptions, which are documented by a large number of examples making up the central part of the book, Courtet is able to identify the following propositions:

1   Living beings are graded in a hierarchy that goes not only from the lower animals to humans, but also divides the human race into defined segments.

2   The various grades correspond to the different races described and classified by physiologists.

3   These racial differences are established not only between distant peoples through their appearance, color, language and other external characters, but also within the society of a nation.

4   In time, racial mixtures occur, producing mixed-race descents, but not so extensively as to eliminate the original characteristics of the primitive types.

5   Since this hybridization between different populations is now the most significant bioanthropic phenomenon, it is clear that knowledge of the ensuing physical and moral results should constitute the essential store of knowledge of the social sciences.

6   Since the races are endowed with organs that are not equally developed – especially as regards the shape and structure of the brain – it follows undeniably that the intellectual faculties of their members will be qualitatively different. Hence the conclusion, presented in the form of a genuine law of nature, since it was confirmed by field observations from historians, travelers, and physiologists: "differences of caste originally go back to differences of race, which, in my mind, leads necessarily to stating that the inequality in the natural power of the races leads to the inequality in their social rank."[25]

Against the various tendencies of modern political philosophy – the absolutist individualism of Hobbes, the radical egalitarianism of Rousseau, the constitutional liberalism of Benjamin Constant, all chosen by Courtet to serve as explicit targets for his critique – what is thus delineated here is a biopolitical anthropology, or an anthropological biopolitics, not just located outside of, but markedly at odds with, the democratic canon and its categories of personal subject, individual will, and equality of conditions. A political science still focused on "issues of people and governments"[26] – already criticized as inadequate by Charles Dunoyer, in a text presented by him as his direct precedent[27] – is replaced by a knowledge of the body and of the species that makes blood the only politically disqualifying element. Of course, the theme of racial difference, already circulating widely in eighteenth-century treatises, is not new in the literature of the period. What marks a turning point, however, and one destined to gain currency and be emphasized in the decades to follow, is the direct use of the anthropological dispositif in political discourse, along with the political modulation of the anthropological contrivance: the concept of *humanitas*, in itself undifferentiated and universal, becomes the specific locus and living material of social selection. In an antinomy typical of this whole line of thought, the hierarchical and exclusionary decision between the various internal types is precisely what is made to characterize the human race as a biological whole. Likewise, bestiality, from the exclusion of which the identity of the species seemed to derive, ends up being included within its ranks. The biological value, and therefore legitimacy – ultimately the right to life – of the races thus becomes measurable on the basis of the proportional relationship between inclusion and exclusion, determined in this fashion: the more one race can be elevated to a higher level, the more the other, or others, will be pushed and relegated to a lower one.

5

If one were to summarize the role played by anthropology in the reciprocal process of drawing implications between politics and biology, one might say that it concerns the transfer of its object – the human being as a living species – from the sphere of history to the sphere of nature. This move – the naturalization of what had always been represented in historical terms – was precisely what enabled the taxonomic placement of the human being in a hierarchical scale that (in its lower ranks at least) included characteristics from the animal world. The human being, or at least its sub-types, can only be animalized if it is first dehistoricized. However, in order for this shift to take place in all its scope and leaving no traces behind, so to speak, it was necessary to overcome an obstacle of no small importance, because it coincided with the essential difference between any type of human being and any type of animal: that is to say, language. While any other human ability can in some way be at least compared, if not identified, with a corresponding capacity in some of the higher animals, this is not true for verbal language, which is proper to the life form called *Homo sapiens*. It is this difficulty – the need to overcome it – that lends the highest strategic importance to another discipline, located at the point of juncture between anthropology and biopolitics, namely linguistics. The observation we made previously about how the mutual exchange between the human sciences has a productive role in bringing about a paradigm shift, in terms of legitimization as well, comes forcefully back into consideration. One might say in this respect that, as anthropology is the semantic commutator that allows politics to model itself on biology, linguistics – more specifically, comparative grammar – constitutes the flow channel for the complete politicization of anthropology.

The origin of this conceptual transfer is the work of the great German linguist August Schleicher, who was first an expert in botany, then a specialist in Slavic languages. His relevance to our inquiry lies not only in the clear naturalistic turn he impressed upon the study of language, but especially in the theoretical path that underlies it, running between Hegel and Darwin. And the most significant aspect of it is not to be found in the transition, explicitly declared, from the influence of Hegel to that of Darwin, as much as in the powerfully ideological effects of their intersection on the relationship between nature and history that underlies the biologization of politics. As has been pointed out by Patrick Tort in his indispensable works,[28] what pushed the overlapping margin between the human sciences and the politics of life in a hierarchical and aggressive direction was not the adoption of the Darwinian paradigm as such, but the prior introduction of the Darwinian paradigm into an analytical and normative framework which preceded it and predisposed it to take a form that was different from its original formulation. Linguistics was a crucial vehicle for this retroactive effect. Already aimed at a genealogical classification of more or less perfect languages at a time when biology was still stuck in a fixist perspective, linguistics was used by Darwin himself as an analogical reference frame for his own model of evolution. But then, the interpretation of language as a continuously evolving, living body dates back to the pre-Romantic tradition of Herder, Humboldt, Schlegel, and their likes. In this framework of broad disciplinary contiguity (also corroborated by the linguistic findings of the geologist Charles Lyell),[29] the turn impressed by Schleicher involves an abrupt passage from metaphor to reality: language is no longer just something organic – because it is characterized by the functional interconnection of all its parts – but a genuine organism with a life of its own, even with respect to those who speak it.

This argument, still framed in Hegelian terms in the first volume of Schleicher's *Comparative Language Studies* in 1848,[30] gains greater clarity in the second volume, published two years later under the title *A Systematic Overview of the European Languages*.[31] At a certain point Schleicher sketches out a sort of auto-critique of his previous outlook, in which he had assumed, following Hegel, that language belongs to the spiritual sphere because it unfolds over the course of history. His intention is not to deny that language undergoes development over time; but it does so in a form that is essentially biological and natural rather than properly historical. What emerges is not an abrupt elimination of the spiritual dimension, but a separation of its function from another, more opaque and heavy sphere, which is, however, considered to be at the same time its original and indispensable root. The point of connection and intersection with the anthropological framework is to be found in this process of articulating through difference. Just as the luminous figure of the human who is fully human – in other words, not also animal – acquires relief only against the dark background of the animal–human, in the same way, something like the spirit of language can only separate itself out of the thick, undifferentiated ground of the biological body. Here are the opening words of the introduction:

> The science which deals with language in general is separated into two distinct branches. One, called *philology*, studies language so that through it we may attain knowledge of the intellectual essence of nationality; philology belongs to history. The other is called *linguistics*; it is in no way concerned with the historical life of nations: it is part of human physiology [...]. The nightingale would never know how to sing like the owl: the same is true for the primitive element of the different human languages.[32]

As was the case for Bichat's biological model of life as a whole, here too, a biologically crucial element like language is identified through the difference that separates it from itself, into two areas, at once autonomous and structured together. In this case, too, they are arranged on the basis of the contrastive relation between will and necessity: to a more external area, characterized by free historical creation, corresponds another, opposing area, folded over upon itself and subject to the iron-clad bond of natural necessity. The latter is the proper object of linguistics. If language as such was the last ontological obstacle to the full naturalization of the animal-human, or human-animal, the science that studies it identifies a primary level whose roots are firmly established in nature.

Schleicher's debt to Darwin, already expressed in the book on the German language,[33] finds its most explicit expression in the two short texts from 1863–4, entitled *Darwinism Tested by the Science of Language*[34] and *The Importance of Language to the Natural History of Man*.[35] In addition to adopting an extreme naturalistic perspective – he finds nothing in language except a biological entity resulting from the activity of phonatory organs and neural terminals – he radically inscribes it within the Darwinian hermeneutic framework. It is true that in Schleicher's epistemic apparatus the creation of a genealogical tree of languages – showing how they descend by gradual changes from a common trunk to differentiate into specific branches – came before his encounter with Darwin. But what was an analogical construct is now endowed with categories (natural selection, struggle for survival, unequal development) that were introduced by the author of the *Origin of the Species*. It is this sudden introduction of what was initially a foreign lexicon – the Darwinian vocabulary – into that of linguistics that caused the latter to come to be directly superimposed in its turn onto the anthropological lexicon. Far from being an insurmountable obstacle to the presence of different bioanthropic thresholds, precisely because it is intimately related to the anatomy of man, language appears to Schleicher as what validates and legitimizes them:

> If language is the specific character of humanity *kat'exochen* [par excellence], this suggests the thought that language might well serve as a principle for distinguishing a scientific and systematic classification of humanity, and form the basis of a natural system of the human genus [...] We have seen that it is mainly language that

distinguishes man as such and that, consequently, the different grades of language must be regarded as the characteristic signs of varying grades of man.[36]

This is the point at which theory of language and anthropology are welded into a single line, defined by the biopolitical emphasis on *clivages* within the human race. The correspondence between the two disciplines, and indeed their mutual functionality, appears to be perfect: as polygenic anthropology – arguing, that is, for a diversified origin of the races – provides a guiding ideological framework for the theory of language, linguistics offers anthropology additional material to test out its differentialist hypothesis. At the center of this encounter, at the point where the two lexicons cross, stands Darwinian biology, taken out of context and put into the heterogeneous semantic framework that came prior to it – Hegelianism – which was never rejected *in toto* and was even used as a general glue for the entire operation. We have already seen how Schleicher did not eliminate the historical dimension in itself, but rather limited it to the practice of philology, focused as this was on the analysis of lexical and literary phenomena. In this way, rather than being unrelated to the sphere of history, language stands in a reversely proportional relationship with it, in the specific sense that it arises from its withdrawal. Indeed, like all other animal organisms, language also undergoes development, which for Schleicher – as it was for Humboldt and the Schlegel brothers – generally consists in a succession: from an early stage of an isolating type, to a next stage of an agglutinating character, culminating finally in an inflectional mode. But – here is the reversal – this movement belongs to the prehistoric era, not to the historical one, where instead the progression gets blocked and turns back on itself into an inevitable decline: the more the phonetic possibilities of modern languages increase, the more their original grammatical wealth diminishes and they are fated to a relentless impoverishment:

From the moment Man begins to recognize himself in what he calls History, he has inevitably ceased to *create* Language, this reflection of his essence; he had created it, but in an era in which he did not yet possess self-awareness. This epoch is beyond any history, evacuated from all memories. Since then, reproduction has taken the place of creation, while there has been increasingly more degeneration in the language groups during the same period.[37]

The relationship is thus fixed: progress is only compatible with non-history, just as history is exclusively bound to decline. It is precisely here that the Darwinian theory of transformism, although clearly in opposition, is siphoned into and subordinated to the ancient theory of degeneration, which was partially adopted even by Hegel. While transformism does not envisage the necessary character of decline – it even presupposes, in principle, a progression from simple to complex – Schleicher translates it into Hegelian terms that reverse the original direction. After modeling the ascending classification of languages on Hegel's hierarchical division of natural history into three parts – namely by making the mineral kingdom correspond to monosyllabic languages, the plant kingdom to agglutinating languages, and the animal kingdom to inflectional languages – he also deduces an implicit evaluative criterion from it. Despite the fact that all modern languages show signs of a progressive degeneration, some of them, starting with the Indo-Germanic, are in any case superior to the others because they have remained stuck at a primitive stage. This is also evident from the superiority of the racial characteristics of the speakers. The short-circuit that comes from the mutual drawing of implications from linguistics to anthropology and vice versa can hardly be avoided at this point.[38] If different languages correspond to different biological structures, language is the best reference for classifying the various human races. But, since different languages have different values, the corresponding races will also necessarily have different values. This is how the biological superiority of certain racial characteristics determined the equally biological superiority of certain languages, while the superior quality of the languages confirmed the superior quality of the races who used them.

## 6

During the same years when Schleicher was pursuing his biolinguistic research, the anthropologist Paul Broca devoted an essay, a critical one actually, to the increasing importance that the sciences of language were gaining for anthropological knowledge.[39] The reason for this involvement is attributed to the fact that knowledge of a language allows one to trace the origins of the population who speaks it, with a perspective into the past that extends back beyond the threshold of history, to root into a still more primordial ground. This is the line of reasoning behind the subtitle *Essay of Linguistic Paleontology*, which Adolphe Pictet chose for his book on the primitive Aryans. There is nothing like linguistic finds to allow us to discover the genesis of what we know only at the stage of its development, since their capacity for preservation is incomparable to that of any other human artifact: "Words last as long as bones; and, just as a tooth implicitly contains a part of the animal's history, one isolated word can furnish indications about the whole series of ideas that are associated with it during its formation."[40] Others, like Max Müller, even compared the deeper layers of the language to those of lava or of the earth's crust, investigated by geology. The point being stressed in both cases, which emphasized the extrahistoric, or at least prehistoric character of language, was how extraneous it is in principle to the voluntary action of people. It is precisely because language escapes the changes of history that it is capable of representing the origin. This also applies to its relation to humans, which is all the more intrinsic at the level of the species as it is weak in terms of consciousness. Rather than speak any given language consciously, human beings are unconsciously 'spoken,' in a form that carves out a hiatus in their subjective identity. Instead of being subjects, people are born subject to the objective constraints of a language that precedes them and determines them in all their conscious activity. Notwithstanding the distinction already established by Schleicher between natural evolution and historical process, language is interpreted by Müller as an independent given, which underlies human experience without being changed by it. Therefore it can reveal something of man's prehistory that not even anthropology is able to penetrate – because, while races cross-pollinate and hybridize over time, language remains faithful to its primary strain. A Celt, argues Müller, can become English, and English blood may contain elements coming from different origins. Not so languages, which are never mixed. The vocabulary and the syntax may be, but certainly not the grammar:

> A student of the language sciences can trace the Celtic, Norman, Greek and Latin ingredients in the English dictionary through their texts, but not a single drop of foreign blood has entered into the organic system of the English language. The grammar, blood, and soul of the language is as pure and intact in the English spoken in the British Isles as it was when it was spoken on the shores of the Germanic sea by the Angles, the Saxons, and the Jutes from the continent.[41]

But the person who ties the structure of a language to the biological substance of the race in an even tighter knot is the Belgian linguist Joseph Honoré Chavée, founder of the *Revue de Linguistique et de Philologie Comparée* and author of a text entitled *Languages and Races*. "Every language," his opening statement declares, "is a natural complement to human organization that is anatomically, physiologically, and psychologically specialized to each race. The characteristic differences in the productive cause (such as the given cerebral–mental organization) are necessarily reflected in the effects produced."[42] This means, he continues, that the Chinese race is to the Chinese language as the Indo-European race is to the Indo-European language. There is nobody who can change this symmetry, from outside or inside these races, since language is an unconscious phenomenon, in every way similar to the digestive system or the circulation of the blood, and thus completely impervious to the commands of free will. To use Bichat's canonical dual division, although language is meant for interhuman communication, its material structure makes it closer to 'organic life' than to 'animal life.' Or, better yet, it represents a third organic layer in its own right, one that is again divided into two: a semantic side, which preserves the soul of the word in a state of perfect integrity; and that of the syllabic body, which is destined to weaken and fall ill, losing "its teeth and hair until it becomes unrecognizable."[43] All languages bear the indelible traces of these illnesses. They, too, are subject to immutable laws, traceable to the degenerative process experienced in the same way by the ethnic groups who speak them. This does not mean, however, that the various languages – like the various races, for that matter – should be located on the same plane. The same logical inconsistency, only heightened, is to be found in Schleicher: all languages degenerate, but some do so more or less slowly than others, because they have an embryonic force that protects them from what is, in any case, an inevitable decline. This is especially true for the only two language races – Aryan or Indo-European and Semitic or Syro-Arab – which have "widely experienced the labor of thought being incarnated into the word."[44]

The thinker that Chavée is explicitly alluding to with these phrases is Ernest Renan. The notion of 'linguistic race' did not only allow him to push the comparison between language and race to the point of eliminating even the marginal difference that Chavée's pupil, Abel Hovelacque (holder of the chair of linguistic anthropology at the École d'Anthropologie), still maintained in his treatise on linguistics, even though he followed in the wake of Schleicher and Müller.[45] It also allowed him to rivet the relationship between languages – and therefore between races – to a comparative framework that did not move it upwards or downwards. Each language remains fixed in a hierarchical position which is determined by its inevitable racial association. This applies to the two noble linguistic races, the Aryan and the Semitic, although they were hardly situated on equal planes either, since the first was receptive to acquisitions from science, art, and politics, while the second remained closed in on itself, incapable of conceiving the multiple, shut off from the future.[46] But it was especially true in the relation, and even more in the contrast, between these two linguistic races and all the others, arranged in a descending hierarchy that sloped gently toward the animal condition.

> As for the inferior races of Africa, Oceania, the New World, and those that preceded the arrival of the Central Asian races almost everywhere, an abyss separated them from the great families: no branch of the Indo-European or Semitic races had descended into savagery. These two races have appeared everywhere with a certain degree of culture. Moreover, there is more than one example of a savage people who has elevated itself to civilization. We must assume that the civilized races never went through a state of sav-

agery and carried with them the seeds of their future progress from the beginning.[47]

What kept the two types of human beings – superior and inferior – at an infinite distance was not only their difference in the present, but also their past and future differences. Just as the superior have no past, the inferior have no future. The superior have always come after the human, while the inferior have always come before the human and continue to do so. Therefore their diversity is not just about race, but about species: they are more than human in one case and less than human in the other.

7

The necessary link between languages and races, developed by the group of linguists gathered around Schleicher, was already at the center of Arthur de Gobineau's grand tableau on *The Inequality of the Human Races*. It might be said that this is the point of both convergence and intensification of all the vectors of meaning identified so far, whose direction leads further and further away from the modern political–philosophical lexicon. The reaction to Gobineau from an author who is anything but orthodox, although still indebted to a conceptual semantics of classical origin, demonstrates this point: "I stop here; allow us, please, to let the discussion rest there. We are separated by too great a space for discussion to be fruitful. There is an intellectual world between your doctrine and mine."[48] The question with which the essay on the races begins is no different from the one posed by Bichat, in his time, regarding the constant presence of death in life and the inexorable sliding of life into death. However, the perspective has been shifted, from the individual to the species – a shift made already by Courtet – and the notion of species has developed in turn according to the presumed difference between the various races. Because "the most obscure, of all the phenomena of history," "so mysterious and so vast in reserve, that the thinker is never weary of looking at it," is not the birth or growth of peoples – "their gains, their conquests, their triumphs" – but the destruction that will sweep them away with such repetitive force that "we are forced to affirm that every assemblage of men, however ingenious the network of social relations that protects it, acquires on the very day of its birth, hidden among the elements of its life, the seed of an inevitable death."[49] The entire book is dedicated to unearthing this degenerative principle: where does it originate from, what fuels it, how does it reproduce? For Gobineau, the difficulty in discovering this principle lies in the fact that it coincides with the ethnic element, in which the life force itself resides. Consequently, those who seek it outside the biological constitution of peoples – in their climate, in the political forms they have provided themselves with, or even in their warring with other peoples – get it wrong, because they fail to grasp that there is nothing capable of overcoming the organic force of the single races other than their own essence, which is vital when the race is intact and weakened at its downfall, when it is mixed with that of other racial strains.

It is here that the author introduces an explicit reference to Bichat, as one who "did not seek to discover the great mystery of existence by studying the human subject from the outside; the key to the riddle, he saw, lay within."[50] The element that emerges most clearly here is not the partial distortion of the position of the French physiologist – who, in reality, sought the most common threat to the continuity of life precisely in the external environment – so much as the slippage, even more important on the biopolitical plane, from the topological distinction between inside and outside to the immunitary distinction between similar and dissimilar, intact and corrupt. What stops the flow of life is not a chance or necessary encounter with a foreign power, but rather its contamination, caused by ethnic crossing between two different racial lines. Even if this sort of *métissage* is necessary for the development of civilization, this does not negate its potentially lethal character. That is why history is, in itself, the principle of death – because it is already conceived in the inherently deadly form of biological existence. This naturalistic transposition of the historical process is perhaps the most distinctive signature of Gobineau's perspective. When he writes that "it is a matter of introducing history into the family of natural sciences,"[51] his intention is more complex than that of simply juxtaposing the languages of biology and history. His aim is rather to translate history itself into the language of the natural sciences. This is made possible through a double homologation that, on the one hand, models historical order on the basis of individual development, while on the other hand it derives individual development from the evolutionary fate of the species. Instead of limiting himself to naturalizing history, it is as if Gobineau had stretched out the segment he had previously dehistoricized over the long duration of humanity's life. A similar relationship arises between matter and spirit: far from being eliminated in favor of materialism, which was foreign to the aristocratic leanings of the author, spirit became the immaterial plane along which organic matter diverges from or adheres to itself; the ideal form from which life grasps the necessity and the structuring of its internal thresholds.

Fifteen years after his book on the races came out, Gobineau published in German a *Memoir on Diverse Manifestations of Individual Life*. In no way reducible to a mere appendage or addendum of his larger work, the *Memoir* is the only explicitly philosophical contribution that the author would make. It is also the work in which the question of the relationship between language and race that was preliminarily sketched out in Chapter 15 of the first section of the *Essai* is drawn out more thoroughly. For good reasons, the editor of the book – which was reissued in a bilingual edition in 1935 – identifies an exact reference to Schleicher, and specifically to his introduction, already commented on here, to the second volume of the *Recherches*, published in French in 1854.[52] From this introduction Gobineau takes the naturalistic interpretation of language as an independent living organism that lies outside the historical dimension. As demonstrated by the superiority of Sanskrit, Greek, and Latin over the modern languages, which he characterizes as increasingly sclerotic and arid in their expressive ability, there is no relationship between the growth of a people's culture and the health of their language. Steady impoverishment of the vocabulary, distortion in the proper functioning of pronouns, progressive atrophy of verbs, reduction in the use of the subjunctive and of the passive voice until they disappear are all tangible signs of the relentless drying up of the primitive language sources. But, if so far Gobineau merely reproduces a model – the critical–degenerative one – widely circulating in Schleicherian comparative grammar, at a certain point he changes his path, opening up a much denser, more peculiar bio-linguistic scenario. At its center stands the problematic – even antinomic – relationship between the three planes of spirit, body, and language, differentiated from each other and yet connected. Generated simultaneously at the birth of a human being, they begin to diverge in the course of its development. Hence it is true that the specific environment of language is the sphere of intelligence or spirit – the German word used by the author is *Geist* – but no one can say that language is a product of spirit. On the contrary, it resides in spirit as a separate, extraneous body:

> The only ground where language can take root is the human spirit; and yet it is a separate being. In the same way, an oak mite would not live on a willow, any more than a willow mite would live on a beech; nevertheless, it is not the tree, in providing the creature with a possibility to live, that created its principle [...] Language is a parasitic body in relation to the spirit.[53]

We must not lose the thread of Gobineau's complex reasoning: there is certainly a point of intersection between spirit and language – located on the interface where words take on their meaning. But this connection in no way diminishes the essential heterogeneity of the two. The 'idiomatic individual' (*idiomatisches Individuum*) – as Gobineau defines the being of language – is essentially external to the structure that houses it. It is ontologically other than the environmental element – the spirit – with which it shares its substance:

> The spirit finds a being within that it did not create, but which lives inside it, and whose substance is similar but not entirely homogeneous to its own; it domesticates the being and makes use of it. It adapts it to its needs as long as it can bend it to itself; it makes language bear the burden; in a word, it treats it as we do the different animal species, upon which we extend our action, but without claiming to have created them or expecting to alter their essential characteristics.[54]

This fundamental lack of homogeneity, this originary alteration of one's identity, is what prevents us from exercising any subjective right on the language we speak, which actually speaks in us. It does not depend in any way on our will – otherwise we would be able to speak any foreign language as we do our own. The fact that this is clearly impossible does not make it certain, says Gobineau, that the cause is a limit to our intelligence. Rather we are prevented by something, by another, more despotic master, which the "idiomatic individual" is bound to in a more compulsory way than it is to the spirit: namely the biological power of the race. This is what expresses the most massive effect of mastery upon that linguistic "parasite," "individual," or "animal" that lives inside us as something other than ourselves: "language holds a similar value to race and reveals a similar organization appropriate to its nature. As long as a race remains pure, its language does not change either, but, when the race undergoes mutations, causing its spirit to change, the language transforms."[55] Unable to influence language directly, the spirit acts as an intermediary between language and race. This intangible intermediary is necessary because, although language is not a product of spirit, it is not a simple phonetic mold of the brain either. Language does not have the same substance as spirit, nor is it a part of the body. This is proven by certain illnesses in which the absence of speech is compatible with a state of perfect physiological health; or, conversely, by diseases in which the dissolution of the body does not lead to a similar crisis in linguistic capacity – at least not until the spirit is also struck dead. In other words, although they are born together, there is no guarantee that spirit, body, and language will die at the same time.

Bichat's principle of splitting life into two forms – organic and animal – returns once again, this time multiplied by three. Contending now for the analytic space are three vital powers, connected and separated by the same membrane that makes one the point of articulation and differentiation between the other two. What determines their integration – or lethal struggle – is their racial correspondence. Only when united by the same race can spirit, body, and language – the three "individuals" that comprise the animal called human – experience their vital power most fully. Life as such – any life, even one that is formless or degraded, with a tendency to degenerate like that of all modern peoples exposed to ethnic hybridization – is always possible; Gobineau still cannot imagine that we can, or should, act on life to extinguish or restrict it. He merely states that "the idiomatic individual born and living in the brain of a common man is never equal to another idiomatic individual which partakes of the attributes of the same race and is attached to a superior person."[56] When Dante is said to have created his own language, the meaning is that he enjoyed the power of an idiomatic being that far surpassed that of other people of his time. It surpassed them by the force of its radiation and intrinsic quality. But it also surpassed them because, like the skin to the body, it adhered to the "genius" of its own race, whose support and guidance are vital to language and without which language degenerates and is impoverished into silence.


## 8

The most influential point of synthesis between Schleicher's bio-linguistic research and later social Darwinism is certainly the work of German zoologist Ernst Haeckel, translator and popularizer of Darwin in Germany. Schleicher's open letter on *Darwinism Tested by the Science of Language*, which we mentioned earlier, was addressed to Haeckel, further illustrating the interweaving of disciplines that provided the terrain and driving force for the paradigm shift taking place during the last decades of the nineteenth and the early decades of the twentieth century. The unique original source of inspiration uniting Haeckel, in addition to Schleicher, to the theologian David Friedrich Strauss, the ethnologist Friedrich Hellwald, and the political philosopher Bartholomäus Carneri was a joint movement that in one direction brought the epistemic status of all other disciplines under the human sciences, while in the other direction it simultaneously pushed the latter into the field of natural sciences.[57] Thus, while linguistics, politics, and even theology – in the particular immanentist version of Strauss – pose questions from the perspective of anthropology, this last discipline is treated in its turn as an integral part of zoology and incorporated as such into the family of natural sciences. As the use of language is not considered at all exclusive to the human species, all the higher functions, including the reasoning capacity, deepen their roots into the world of animals. When Haeckel, articulating what has been defined as the fundamental law of biogenetics, states that ontogeny recapitulates phylogeny – in other words, the history of the individual reproduces on a smaller scale the history of the species – he means that what appears to us as historical progress is in reality the predetermined outcome of natural evolution. This does not mean – as in Schleicher's case – that Haeckel excludes what is commonly known as spirit, or soul, from the scope of his observation. On the contrary, he includes it beforehand within the general physical–chemical process out of which a particular type of animal, who gave itself the name of 'human,' arose at a given time. Ethical or religious attitudes, too, anything but eternal values or inner standards deriving from a categorical imperative, are the functional result of the struggle for survival in which the entire organic world is engaged.

The 180-degree turn that the concept of politics takes with respect to all its possible modern forms is evident from these sorts of assumptions. From this point of view, Haeckel's refusal to adopt a specific position in the ideological struggle of his time – he declared himself to be anti-socialist, but also anti-liberal; and anti-reformist, but at the same time anti-traditionalist – should be interpreted as the result of a radical rupture with the previous philosophical and political framework rather than as an essentially impolitic attitude. It is easy to understand why, then, taking up and developing Courtet's reasoning in a more intensely biologistic key, Haeckel maintained that the unfortunate evils of contemporary politics

> are due to the fact that most of our officials are jurists – that is, men of high technical education, but utterly devoid of that thorough knowledge of human nature which is only obtained by the study of comparative anthropology and the monistic psychology – men without an acquaintance with those social relations of which we find the earlier types in comparative zoology and the theory of evolution, in the cellular theory, and the study of the protists.[58]

Against the idea, implicit in the modern philosophical paradigm, that political activity is an expression of the conscious will of rational individuals who, as legal persons, possess a series of subjective rights that make them somehow masters of their own

destiny, there begins to emerge the idea of the determination of
the will, but also its substitution with an even more indissoluble
bond, the hereditary transmission of natural traits:

> We now know that each act of the will is as fatally determined by
> the organization of the individual and as dependent on the momen-
> tary condition of his environment as every other psychic activity.
> The character of the inclination was determined long ago by *hered-
> ity* from parents and ancestors; the determination to each particular
> act is an instance of *adaptation* to the circumstances of the moment
> wherein the strongest motive prevails, according to the laws which
> govern the statics of emotion. Ontogeny teaches us to understand
> the evolution of the will in the individual child. Phylogeny reveals
> to us the historical development of the will within the ranks of our
> vertebrate ancestors.[59]

This opens up the avenue toward that radical depersonalization
which leads ultimately to the crushing of the identity of the subject
into its bare biological and racial given. But the element that
makes Haeckel's anthropology a true predecessor of the thanatopolitical drift of the following decades is its breach of continuity
in the series of human races, operated through the insertion of the
animal within that series, as a point of reference. The animal –
explicitly breaking even with the Darwinian paradigm, which had
also formed the epistemological framework of Haeckel's monism
– no longer constitutes the place of origin of the human species,
but the measure of its internal difference. Hence, after a detailed
description of the various races on the basis of hair type, skin
color, and shape of the skull – which forms a hierarchy going from
*homo australis* through *homo mongolicus* up to the Caucasian
and Indo-Atlantic – we learn that the higher animals are closer to
humans than to other lower animals, but also that the lower
humans are more similar to animals than to the higher humans.
This means that domesticated animals, or animals that can be
domesticated, are located in the hierarchy of living species between
primitive races and civilized races – and that therefore *humanitas*
is split into two distinct parts, set off from each other by a transversal line formed by reference to the animal. The animal is not
the origin of the human species, but rather the line of separation
inscribed within the human species.

If we are to draw a sharp boundary between them, it must be drawn between the most highly developed and civilized man on the one hand, and the rudest savages on the other, and the latter have to be classed with the animals. This is, in fact, the opinion of many travellers who have long watched the lowest human races in their native countries. [They say:] "I consider the negro to be a lower species of man, and cannot make up my mind to look upon him as 'a man and a brother,' for the gorilla would then also have to be admitted into the family." [...] [I]t would be easier to train the most intelligent domestic animals to a moral and civilized life, than these unreasoning brute-like men [...] They stand far below unreasoning animals.[60]

The outcome of this biopolitical decision – located at the point of intersection and overlap between the humanization of the higher animals and the animalization of the lower humans – is clear. The Indo-Germanic peoples already triumphed all over the world thanks to the biological power of their brain development.

But the other races, which as it is are very much diminished in number, will sooner or later completely succumb in the struggle for existence to the superiority of the Mediterranean races [...] The American and Australian tribes are even now fast approaching their complete extinction, and the same may be said of the Dravidas, Papuans, and Hottentots.[61]

## 9

In Haeckel, anthropology already assumes a role of objective opposition to the set of categories that converge in the definition of modern democracy. This is in harmony, not at odds, with its inherent extraneity to the lexical sphere traditionally assigned to politics. The criterion of equality is invalidated not by a different concept of society, but in the name of a biological given closer to origins and more aggressive, which forms the ontogenetic backdrop. As Haeckel writes in *Freedom in Science and Teaching*, the law of natural selection itself is anything but democratic, since it saves a few while condemning the majority to destruction.[62] What is radically questioned, more than any ideological option, is the whole political horizon of modernity, beginning with the very concept of legal person – on the one hand crushed into its bodily substrate, and on the other deprived of individuality by being massed up in the indistinctness of species or race. But an even clearer step in the direction of thanatopolitics takes place when, instead of opposing it from outside the political sphere, the discipline of anthropology incorporates the operational, literally decision-making value of politics, defining itself precisely as 'political anthropology' or 'socio-anthropology.' These are exactly the terms that appear in the titles of two books destined to play a leading role in the paradigmatic transformation of anthropological thought at the turn of the century: *The Social Order and Its Natural Foundations: An Outline of Social Anthropology Dealing with Social Issues for Use by the Educated*, by Otto Ammon,[63] and *Political Anthropology: A Study of the Influence of the Theory of Descent on the Doctrine of the Political Development of Peoples*, by Ludwig Woltmann.[64]

The critical threshold that separates these terms from Haeckel's anthropology – still locatable, albeit with some straining, within Darwinism – is closely related to the reception of the germ plasma theory, developed by August Weismann. This theory holds that natural selection does not act at the somatic level of the phenotype, but at the more profound level of the genotype. This assumption – the idea that generations are united in time by the unbroken continuity of the same blood – burns all bridges with Lamarck's notion of the ability of acquired characteristics to be transferred genetically, a notion confusingly mingled with the teachings of Darwin and used, especially in socialist circles, as proof of environmental influence on the formation of character. The only mutation now possible appears to be a degenerative one, which occurs due to racial hybridization. Although Weismann, like Gregor Mendel later, is not responsible for the biopolitical or thanatopolitical use of his discovery, what the German anthropology of the time concludes from it is the need to halt the process of degeneration by restoring the shattered natural order, perverted first through the mixing of races and next through the mechanisms of social protection aimed at defending the weaker organisms. The concept of 'artificial selection' (*Auslese*), still linked to that of 'inheritance' (*Vererbung*), is well suited for this purpose.[65] But what is even

more important – because it conveys a sense of the brusque reversal made by the new anthropology – is the fact that this notion is
now adopted directly against the use that Darwin made of it a few
decades earlier. While in Darwin's view artificial selection, as put
into practice by farmers and breeders, was intended to cross plant
and animal species existing in nature for the artificial creation of
a better type, for these authors the time has come to put an end
to any blood mixtures in order to recover the original types. If, in
the case of Darwin, it was a matter of going beyond nature in
some way, forcing it to take an unnatural direction, the aim
pursued by German anthropologists was to use artificial means in
order to recreate a nature that had been lost or perverted. But the
project, in itself contradictory, of artificially re-naturalizing nature
– of regenerating the natural through the artificial – was only possible through a negative approach: by first excluding and then
removing organisms that were degenerate or destined for
degeneration.

Georges Vacher de Lapouge – the French editor of Haeckel's
book on monism – who published his own essays on 'anthroposociology' a few years later under the title *Race and Social Background*, traces out precisely this argument. Starting from the
canonical reference to Gobineau as a precursor of racial theory,
he splits off from him in the name of a different scientific attitude,
matured thanks to the discoveries of Mendel and Weismann. On
the basis of these authors, and against the illusory Lamarckian
assumptions of transformism, the concept of blood inheritance has
brought anthroposociology to the status of a true science, he
states. From this point on, race is no longer to be interpreted in
a metaphorical and literary way, as a community of culture or
destiny, but in a directly zoological fashion, amenable to the
nomenclature established by Carl Linnaeus. There are two types
prevalent in Europe, measurable by means of the cephalic index
and by defining their somatic and character traits: *homo euro-
paeus*, dolichocephalic, long-headed, energetic, and courageous;
and *homo alpinus*, brachycephalic, round-headed, sedentary, and
not very enterprising. The entire history of the civilized world is
the result of the confrontation, or struggle, between these two
races and the intermediate ones, such as the Mediterranean race,
in whom the original traits have been mingled. The conclusion

Vacher de Lapouge draws, in reference to modern political philosophy, is that a clash with democracy cannot be avoided: "It is certain, however, that contemporary biology stands in absolute antinomy to democratic ideas. I refer to biology and not anthroposociology, because the concepts at the base of the conflict are borrowed by anthroposociology from biology."[66] From this point of view, the political is fully embedded in the biological, not only because the object of the struggle is life itself, but also because it is never individual or socio-cultural, but always – ultimately – ethnic and racial. The individual, understood as the subject made equal to others through the faculty of free will or the ownership of individual rights, does not exist as such, except as an epiphenomenon of a difference that is absolute because it relates to the germ plasma circulating in our bodies. The breaking point in modern history, when development was reversed into deterioration, was the French Revolution, when the supremacy of the Aryan type over the Alpine was overturned, giving an advantage to the latter that resulted in long-term degenerative effects. This is why Vacher de Lapouge replied to the revolutionary motto 'Liberty, Fraternity, Equality' with the otherwise threatening formula 'Determinism, Inequality, Selection.'[67] The implicit biothanatological assumption is all too obvious: if the natural purity of the race has been corrupted through blood, it can only be restored through the shedding of blood: "Forget the fraternity, woe to the vanquished. Life is preserved only through death."[68]

## 10

The dialectic that Bichat had established as the origin of the philosophy of life returns, but its direction has been reversed. Death is no longer the unavoidable background, or continuous challenge, out of which life emerges and against which it exerts resistance, but the primary instrument of its preservation and enhancement. The conceptual and operational locus where this reversal takes form is the concept – or, more precisely, the 'practice' – of humanity. Contrary to what one might expect, with the rising tide of Nazism the notion of humanity, rather than narrowing its borders, gradually expanded so as to encompass its opposite. Hence the increasingly important role of anthropology, strengthened and reinforced first by linguistics and then, progressively, by zoology and botany. It is no accident that the terms it used in order to refer to human beings were increasingly drawn from the vocabulary of these disciplines: 'selection,' as we have discussed, but also 'domestication' (*Zähmung*), 'breeding' (*Züchtung*), 'cultivation' (*Anbau*): all, procedures whose final outcome involves the 'eradication' *(Ausmerzung)* of the defective products. What Vacher de Lapouge called 'anthroposociology' is increasingly confused with human–animal zootechnics, in which the human must be surgically separated from time to time from the animal that inhabits it. The selection technique may vary in this procedure, but not the 'material' character of its object. Not because reference is no longer made to form, shape, or idea – constantly extolled as the ultimate goal of the racially perfect human being – but because it is always made in contrast – and indeed in inverse proportion – to another type, or counter-type, defined by its original deformation or by the absence of form, which reduced it to simple living material.[69] In this respect we can say that, for Nazi anthropozoology, *humanitas* is the line, continually being revised, along which life is separated from itself into two opposite polarities that require each other for their functioning – to the extent that the excess form of one is complementary to, and hence consequent upon, the absolute deformalization of the other. Never as in this case had *bios* and *zoe* (form of life and formless life) diverged so as to situate themselves at such an irremediable distance from each other. Irremediable because it is constituted by an inverse or direct relation with death: on the one hand, a life so alive that it can present itself as immortal; on the other, a life that is no longer such – "existence without life" (*Dasein ohne Leben*), as it was called – because it is contaminated and perverted by death from the outset.

When we take a look at the numerous books on the topic of humanity that were published around the 1930s in Germany and other countries, they form a shocking snapshot, all coming from the same drift. Vacher de Lapouge, mindful of the more sinister teachings of Haeckel, devoted an entire section of his *Sélections* to the necessary elimination of human types that were defective, and therefore harmful to society as a whole. It was in the name of humanity that Nobel Prize winner Charles Richet, also in a book on *Sélection humaine*, stated that "a mass of human flesh without human intelligence is nothing. It is living material that is unworthy of any respect or compassion."[70] Similarly, another Nobel Prize winner, Alexis Carrel, in the chapter on "The Remaking of Man" in his celebrated book *Man the Unknown*, recommended that

> those who have murdered, robbed while armed with automatic pistol or machine gun, kidnapped children, despoiled the poor of their savings, misled the public in important matters, should be humanely and economically disposed of in small euthanasic institutions supplied with proper gases. A similar treatment could be advantageously applied to the insane, guilty of criminal acts. Modern society should not hesitate to organize itself with reference to the normal individual. Philosophical systems and sentimental prejudices must give way before such a necessity. The development of human personality is the ultimate purpose of civilization.[71]

On the other hand Alfred Hoche's essay on "life unworthy of life," co-written with Karl Binding, warned of "an inflated concept of humanity,"[72] such that we fail to understand how inhumane it is to apply the same treatment to types of humans who are essentially (in other words, biologically) different. This was the latest, but also the first argument brought to its theoretical maturity by the Nazi "philosopher" Hans Günther, in a text appropriately called *Humanitas* and distributed widely to all the Hitler Youth as a handbook of applied ethics. Speaking against the reduction of humanism by Levantine immigrants, especially Jews, to "a doctrine of brotherhood and equality, in the name of an abstract, non-existent human being," Günther claims that true *humanitas* is not a given, but

> a task to fulfill, a model to achieve [...] an ideal of racial selection and marriage, because only a concept that distinguishes between the best and the worst can retain a real ethicality and ideality, an aristocratic concept [...] a concept that is the knowledge of better blood that needs to be increased and of worse blood, from which we should not wish to have numerous offspring.[73]

The path that leads from the knowledge of life – conceived of for a very different purpose at the beginning of the previous century – to the most lethal practice of death has been fully accomplished. Only when its meaning and direction are reversed into its opposite – what is defined as biopolitics, in the sense of an originary implication between politics and life – does it express its extreme thanatological capacity, under Nazism. At its core, or in its origin, as we have seen, there is the clear-cut substitution of the idea of person with the idea of the human body in which the person is biologically rooted. The living creature called a human being, in this case reduced to its bare determination of race or species, is what remains after the destruction of the personal form – or after the abolition of the 'mask' – with which this creature had been vested by modern political philosophy. When the Nazis claimed for themselves the right to act decisively on the biological continuum of the species to rescue it from its incipient degeneration, they brought this project, already taken up by the German anthropology of the time, to its final outcome of stripping the living body of any formal mediation in order to make it the object of a political decision. Naturally, any political system like Nazism, which deals directly with human bodies, cannot differ in its healing intention from a form of medicine based on racial surgery. This is the final lexical overlap – after biology, anthropology, linguistics, and zoology – to which political knowledge was subjected, in a form that gave the "great German physician," as the Führer proclaimed himself, the exalted task of proceeding with the prescribed amputation: no longer to be performed on individuals but on that great body of humanity into which, for some time now, they had been swallowed up.[74]

## 11

One of the most effective tools used in the Nazi deconstruction of the person was language. The German Jewish philologist Victor Klemperer, who survived the genocide only thanks to his marriage with an 'Aryan' woman, reconstructed and documented the language transformation process conducted by the Nazis.[75] More than a simple ideological conversion undertaken for the purposes of the new power, it was a veritable poisoning of speech that gradually infected all strata of German society. It is as if, by actively participating in the annihilation of individual freedom, and then of the individuals themselves, language became prey to its own destructive power, gradually sliding into a sort of vortex. What got pulled down into this maelstrom was the natural metaphoric richness of the language, its plurivocality of meaning, its historical depth, its very signifying capacity, which was muddied and then, increasingly, nullified by the obvious desire to extinguish any critical attitude and eventually the possibility of thought itself. Recorded in the official statements of the Nazi leaders, but also in the ordinary communication of those who were affected – almost all Germans, in effect – was the continued quantitative and qualitative reduction of the lexicon to a single function, amounting to the subordination of an entire people to the criminal intention of those who had enslaved it. There was no need to create new expressions to accomplish this goal: it sufficed to twist existing ones in a different, or even opposing, direction. Thus, while some more complex expressions considered unusable (if not harmful) disappeared, others, converted into slogans and regressive watchwords, were indelibly imprinted into the soul or, more accurately, into the bodies of the chosen race. In this way language, mutilated and distorted, became a hidden force helping to guide the conduct of the people in a form that escaped their rational control and conscious will. From this point of view, the irrational and involuntary nature of language and its progressive degeneration, theorized by Schleicher and his successors, were both verified. Except for the minor detail that, according to these linguists, the 'Indo-German' language should have avoided, or at least slowed down, the degenerative process that was taking place rather than bringing it to completion. What, starting from Hegel, was supposed to be the philosophical language par excellence, because in its most meaningful expressions it could accommodate the power of contradiction, ultimately revealed itself to be most antithetical to the exercise of creative thought.

The place where, more than in any other, the German language disclosed – and also produced – this effect of depersonalization was undoubtedly the concentration camp. In it, the reduction of the communicative function to the harshness of a command, to the brutality of a threat, to the vulgarity of a curse reached its apex. Almost nothing associated with the language of Goethe and Heine remained in the shouted word, the strangled cry, or the chaotic, formless barking that accompanied the deportees from the time of their arrival at the camps until their death. More than communicating content, or even informing someone about something, the words affected the bodies of the victims in the same way as the number printed on their arm or the blows delivered to their limbs. Not by chance, at Mauthausen a truncheon was called 'the interpreter' (*der Dolmetscher*), because it was the most direct translation tool for those who did not understand German. All this was an integral part of the complete bestialization of the prisoners: "This was a signal," says Primo Levi, "for those people we were no longer men. With us as with cows or mules, there was no substantial difference between a scream and a punch."[76] Thus, when referring to eating activities involving the prisoners, as minimal as they were, the verb used was *fressen*, normally used to describe animal feeding, rather than *essen*, commonly applied to human beings. The act of hunting down or killing prisoners, performed far more frequently by the jailors, was defined by words for exterminating hares, rabbits, and mice, taken from the hunting jargon: mangled, chopped, baked flesh. If the inmates were beasts, however, they were also and above all things. The language conveyed and at the same time determined this reification through *Akkusativierung*, reduction of the nominative to the accusative case. Instead of talking about men and women, they referred to pieces (*Stücke*), replacement parts (*Häftlinge*), human material (*Menschenmaterial*), to be loaned (*ausleihen*), unloaded (*abladen*), shipped (*verschiffen*), and eventually, of course, destroyed, after the recovery of the recyclable parts.[77]

But the effect that was in some ways even more devastating than this 'linguistic turn' was its power of contaminating those to whom it was addressed. All those who escaped death have recounted how they themselves came to adopt a way of speaking that was no different in lexical structure and basic register from that of their would-be killers. This stemmed primarily from the fact that the majority of them were not Germans and therefore could not express themselves except in the curt, violent language that they heard – or rather felt on their body like lashes. This confirms the claim of those[78] who spoke of a genuine 'camp language,' a *Lagersprache* (or *Lagerszpracha* in Polishized German) – something similar to the special languages (*Sondersprachen*) that cover the three different functions of a secret jargon, a technical jargon, and a group jargon. The language of the camp had the peculiarity of uniting all these functions together in the same 'order of discourse': while it was necessary in addressing certain situations that required specific skills, it was also useful for communicating with other prisoners of different nationalities and, where possible, for passing secret information to the outside world. In some cases, precisely because it adhered to the expressive mode of the executioners, it allowed them to escape from their grip, offering escape routes from the more immediate risks. Not surprisingly, then, Levi maintains that *Lagersprache* – the ability to establish contact with the SS, by using their own linguistic modules, naturally – was the most precious treasure one could have in these circumstances, to the extent that knowing or not knowing the language often determined whether a prisoner escaped death or was swallowed up by it, as happened regularly to those who were slow to learn it. The tendency of the survivors, reported on several occasions, to return to that degraded, vile language when they met again after the war is perhaps attributable to the same circumstances. Whatever the reason may be, there is no doubt that it was difficult to get rid of what they had learned in the hell out of which they emerged. So much so that Levi recounts how he often had to argue with his own translators when they insisted on deleting or urbanizing the crude expressions he faithfully reported from his *Lagerjargon*:

> I explained to them [some Bayer employees] that I hadn't learned German at school, but in a Lager called Auschwitz [...] I later on realized also that my pronunciation is coarse, but I deliberately have not tried to make it more genteel; for the same reason, I have never had the tattoo removed from my left arm.[79]

How can this loyalty to a ghost, one that everything would make you want to forget, or at least, avoid reviving, be explained? Why be attached to the camp language, as if it were a piece of your skin or a bodily organ? The most obvious answer is that you want to witness the existence of this inverted world whose contours tend over time to become hazy or even lose their plausibility to those who had no direct knowledge of it. By preserving the language of the camps, the survivors attest to its historical reality, to the death sentence it expressed to millions of people. My impression, however, is that this is only one part of the truth. This skeletal, satanic language, inside and beyond death, more than anything also recalls the life that has been torn from it. *Lagersprache* was both the language of the murderers as well as the language of survival for the victims who escaped their fate. Not, as has been suggested, because it still bore a certain "feeling of life," but because it was bare, material expression of life without feeling of those who were no different from it: the language of men and women who no longer qualified as persons, precisely because they were perfectly adherent to the biological layer of their mere being in existence. From this other point of view, it is something that points to the biological nature of the language in a previous modality, or later, to the personal and even specifically human form of the individual. Never as much as in this case might it be said – as the Romantic linguists expressed it – that the people did not speak the language; rather, they were spoken by the language without being able to master it. But they did so with a diametrically opposed valence that recalls instead the persistence of organic life, beyond animal life, described by Bichat. Even for the inmates in the camp, the life-language or language-life was something absolutely common to all those who, regardless of their different backgrounds, spoke it and survived only by speaking it. In its complete impersonality, it was life-*with* – the only way of living together that was possible, while it lasted – but also life-*against* all that besieged it from all sides, trying literally to send it up in smoke. It was resistance to death, when not only human life but also animal life had already surrendered to its pressure.

# 2

# Person, Human, Thing

---

## 1

Even before the war ended, the perception had spread that there
was a close link between what made Nazism utterly different and
its deadly use of the category of 'humanity.' Unlike all previous
regimes that were directed toward the development of a particular
model of society, the chosen object of Nazism's thanatopolitical
grip was human nature as such. Not surprisingly, then, when the
Allied victory became apparent and along with it the possibility
of bringing Nazi leaders to justice, the most urgent task to be
performed, even before attempting any legal definition, was the
conceptual development of a notion of 'crimes against humanity.'
What, exactly, is a crime committed against humanity as a whole,
and what form does it take by comparison to other types of crime?
The answer to this question, obviously preliminary to any other
consideration, was not easy to arrive at, because it lay in areas
marginal to, or even outside of, the scope of the law. The difficulties involved were two. First, it was as if the concept of humanity
presented some secret resistance, a sort of semantic incompatibil-
ity with respect to legal language. Second, even more embarrass-
ingly, the concept seemed somehow involved, and therefore guilty
before charged, in the vocabulary of those who, while twisting
and perverting its meaning to the point of abasement, had been

the first to make it the object of a direct political decision. Perhaps this hidden complicity was what lay behind the victors' temptation to resolve the issue of punishing the guilty irrespective of any legal process – an urge they resisted only with some reluctance and out of fear of being widely discredited. The US Attorney General expressed the hope that what was called in Texas "the law West of Pecos," a kind of legalized lynching, would be applied to Nazi war criminals, while Churchill thought they should be eliminated within six hours of being caught. His advisor for legal affairs and Lord Chancellor, John Simon (aptly expressing an extrajudicial attitude that was symmetrical in some ways to the state of permanent exception established by the Nazis) proposed that those who had placed themselves outside all legal constraints should be made, literally, 'outlaws.' The precedent he drew on was a provision in medieval Britain authorizing a grand jury to declare anyone who was guilty of particularly heinous crimes a 'bandit,' in other words an 'outlaw,' without going through court proceedings. Once declared to be outside the law, such people could be legally killed by anyone who captured them, which is exactly what happened to Jews in Nazi Germany. In the fourteenth century this right to perform summary executions, originally extended to all citizens, was restricted to the local sheriff. Now, since British law had repealed the outlaw status in the sphere of criminal law only a few years earlier, Simon's view was that in these circumstances the Allies could be regarded as equivalent to a grand jury and their senior officers to a sheriff, with respect not only to Nazi leaders but to everyone considered to be their accomplices. In this spirit Clement Attlee, leader of the Labour Party, made a proposal to execute a number of German industrialists "as an example to others."[1]

Even when these sorts of options were abandoned in favor of trial proceedings, the technical and conceptual difficulties were still not resolved. On the contrary, although the concept of a crime against humanity was clearly the cutting edge of the entire prosecutory apparatus, the more closely the issue was examined, the more thorny the difficulties became. At first the concept was included into the more traditional one of 'war crime'; but, because it differed in some essential traits, starting from the fact that a crime against humanity could be committed in peacetime (as had happened in Germany from 1933 to 1939), it was given a status of its own in the Charter of the International Military Tribunal. Perhaps the most explosive aspect of the new formulation was that, for the first time ever, an entire country could be charged for crimes committed against its own citizens. This meant extending to individuals the same legal subjectivity that until then had only been granted in international law to state organisms. Article 6 of the Charter made the jurisdiction of the Tribunal independent from the law of the countries in which the crime was committed, while the next two articles rescinded the mitigating circumstances of the defendant's official position or any actions performed in obedience to a superior in his or her organization or government. In short, crimes against humanity escaped the spatio-temporal constraints that had hitherto governed the legal procedures of individual nations.[2] But precisely this fact led to several problems that were not easy to resolve as long as one remained within the confines of the usual juridical categories – especially with regard to national sovereignty, which was now threatened by a potentially unlimited right of interference. If a foreign court could indict the autonomous government of a sovereign state for crimes committed not only against the international community, but also against its own citizens, this would allow a war to be waged against any nation in the name of unwritten laws considered implicit to humankind simply by nature and by custom. To claim that certain crimes are so far removed from the normal that they cannot be provided for before they are committed, as was indeed claimed, was tantamount to placing crimes against humanity on a receding horizon – but also a conflicting one – vis-à-vis positive law.

To avoid this extrajudicial consequence, the tribunals that had recourse to the concept of crimes against humanity after the Nuremberg trials appealed to the Universal Declaration of Human Rights adopted by the United Nations in December of 1948. This was the only way they could oppose to the prerogative of national sovereignty a higher legal value, which consisted in the personal right of every individual member of humankind. And yet it was this specific reference that ended up creating the most glaring contradiction in the new doctrine. While Article 11 of the Declaration proclaims the principle of the non-retroactivity of the penal offence, stating that nobody can be punished in accordance with a law enacted after the crime was committed, the notion of crime against humanity, as was applied in Nuremberg, reversed that logical order by placing the crime before the law that sanctioned it. The gap that appeared from the outset to separate the category of humanity from that of legal right thus risked widening rather than narrowing. The individual right given to every person in the Declaration of 1948 does not correspond to the concept of crimes against humanity in the same way a positive does to a negative. Instead of one being the reverse of the other, their logics diverge in an irreconcilable fashion. What holds true for the individual is not true for humankind, and vice versa. No matter how they are conceptualized, the three terms 'individual,' 'law,' and 'humanity' fail to line up along a single path. Each seems to stand in the way of the other two at the junction where these two meet up. Law is incapable of uniting humanity and the individual. Individuals cannot find recognition of themselves as human beings in the dispositif of the law.

## 2

Never more than today has the notion of 'human rights' appeared more riddled with an obvious contradiction. Its growing success in terms of declarations – attested to by the continuing proliferation of conventions inspired by these rights – is offset by a more pronounced lack of confidence in their effective implementation. Initially proclaimed in the Declaration of 1789, human rights experienced their greatest success at the end of the Second World War, for the reasons we have just examined: at a time when humanity as a whole (rather than a single people) had been targeted, a response in its name to any other present or future threat was seen as essential. And yet the solemn and explicit formulation of the right of every person to an appropriate form of life is precisely what has made the continuing violation of this principle all the more evident. This gap seemed to become invincible in 2006, when the world received the incredible news that several countries that had distinguished themselves in recent years through their systematic devastation, such as Pakistan and Saudi Arabia, had become members of the United Nations Human Rights Council. Hence the gradual formation of a critical attitude, which has split into three distinct but compatible lines of argument.[3] According to the first, which is of Marxist descent, human rights are nothing more than an ideological cover for the political and economic imperialism of the great powers, pursued at the expense of regimes that are not aligned with their interests. The second line, inspired by historicism, challenges the universal character of demands that are continually evolving, often at odds with each other, tied to specific historical contexts and situations, and hence irreducible to a fixed, universally valid catalog. The third line has a realist leaning: while accepting in principle the validity of human rights legislation, it denounces its impracticality in a world still suspended between global dynamics and the sovereign power of individual states.

My impression, however, is that none of the angles adopted from these perspectives really make deep inroads into the question; they all somehow skirt around the phenomenon. This is not to deny that the issues they engage with truly exist; however, by isolating one or the other from the entirety of the problem, these critiques lose sight of the whole and wind up confusing the cause with the effect. The kernel of meaning that is obscured (or at least muddied) by these approaches is the aporia inherent in the concept of human rights. What I mean by this is not the line of tension between ideology and reality, universal and particular, or prescription and description – which is highlighted by each proponent in turn – but the line that passes between the two terms of the expression – between rights and the human condition – and in the process rips them apart. The only thinker who has come close to tackling the question, although without fully exploring its ramifications, is Hannah Arendt. In one section of *The Origins of Totalitarianism* she discusses "The Decline of the Nation State and the End of the Rights of Man." The reason why human rights have come to their end, she says, is not the inability to follow in practice what was proclaimed in theory – the weakness of a law lacking adequate enforcement – but something deeper: namely, a dispositif inherent in the juridical form itself. The problem is not that the law, for contextual or external reasons, fails to protect people when they are deprived of any quality other than the mere fact of being human. The problem is that its very functioning does not provide for this condition – or, better still, does not prevent it. In this way a human being, understood in the most basic sense, is excluded from the benefits of the law – deprived of rights, in other words – not in spite of being such but *because* of it:

> The conception of human rights [...] broke down at the very moment when those who professed to believe in it were for the first time confronted with people who had indeed lost all other qualities and specific relationships – except that they were still human. If a human being loses his political status, he should, according to the implications of the inborn and inalienable rights of man, come under exactly the situation for which the declarations of such general rights provided. Actually the opposite is the case. It seems that a man who is nothing but a man has lost the very qualities which make it possible for other people to treat him as a fellow-man.[4]

At the core of this contradiction – causing human rights to implode precisely at the moment when they should have their greatest force – Arendt detects an anomaly in the juridical procedure as such. At its center stands the structurally exclusive mechanism of rights, which are inclusive through exclusion. Although she connects their most conspicuous emergency to a specific historical situation, characterized by the nationalistic conversion of the European states and by the growing masses of stateless persons who were put into circulation as a result, Arendt identifies a constant inherent to the regulatory structure: this is the prior assumption of a boundary between what lies inside and what remains outside its sphere of action. From the juridical point of view, the 'inside,' the measure of inclusion, is defined only by contrast to what is outside, what is not included in its parameters. Now, against all the rhetoric, past and future, on the humanity of the law, the human being as such is precisely what law excludes from within its borders: what Arendt calls the "abstract nakedness of being human and nothing but human."[5] Although she does not offer a thorough analysis of the logic and workings of this dispositif, she does capture the full range of its perplexity: the law allows entrance only to those who fall into some category – citizens, subjects, even slaves – hence, insofar as they are part of a political community.

For those who have been excluded because they do not fall into any category, therefore, the only way to get back inside is negative: by breaking the law rather than by complying with it. In other words, since the law will not admit them through any positive avenue, their only option is to violate it. Only this way, by voluntarily taking on the status of a criminal, by losing a state of innocence that is impossible to keep because the law does not recognize it, can someone with no other prerogatives come to enjoy at least the rights granted even to offenders: "As a criminal even a stateless person will not be treated worse than another criminal, that is, he will be treated like everyone else. Only as an offender against the law can he gain protection from it."[6] At least as long as the trial lasts and the punishment continues, he can leave the zone of juridical haziness in which the status of 'no-more-than-human being' has placed him, to become a citizen again like everyone else, in spite of being condemned for a crime somehow imposed on him by the same law that punishes him for it.

## 3

The concept of 'person' was intended to fill in the chasm opened up between the poles of human being and citizen that had existed since the Declaration of 1789. If we compare this text to the Universal Declaration of Human Rights of 1948, the difference is plain to see: the new semantic epicenter, shifting away from the revolutionary emphasis on citizenship, is the unconditional demand for the dignity and worth of the human person. The reason for this substitution lies partly in the need to remove rights from the necessarily restricted limits of the nation; but the substitution also reflects the peculiar ability of the term 'person' to summarize, in a single word, elements and echoes deriving both from the culture of the Enlightenment and from theological language. One would be hard put to come up with a concept in the corpus of the Western tradition that has an equally dual character, simultaneously secular and religious: 'person' has signified the divine Trinity ever since the Christian lexicon was invented, but also the subject of law as a bearer of rational will. The passageway, or point of tangency, from one sphere to the other is the concept of natural law, which up to a certain point (essentially coinciding with Spanish neoscholasticism) was still subordinated to a supernatural principle; only later, beginning with Hobbes, was it brought back entirely to its earthly roots. Now, what explains the centuries-old success of the term 'person' is not that it was eventually freed from its Christian lien; on the contrary, its success is based precisely on this Christian resonance, which has persisted throughout modern secularization. Even when interpreted in secular terms, in short, the idea of person is never entirely reducible to that of the biological substrate of the subject it designates; rather, its most significant meaning is to be found precisely in a sort of excess, of a spiritual or moral character, that makes more of the 'person,' yet without letting it coincide completely with the self-sufficient individual of the liberal tradition. It is actually the locus of their most intense combination: the inseparable relationship between body and soul in a single entity, open to relationship with other persons.

This element of ulteriority with respect to the bare corporeal given was first subject to deconstruction and then to thorough destruction by the biopolitical tradition we have reconstructed in the previous chapter by showing its assumptions, development, and finally its deadly reversal, carried out under Nazism with calamitous results. What was gradually chipped away at, until shattering completely, was precisely this transcendental unity of will and reason that modern political philosophy had relied on to allow human beings the ability to consciously choose their preferred model of shared life. Already the separation initially established by Bichat between the two types of life – organic and animal – with the quantitative and temporal dominance of the first over the second, had disrupted the idea of the person as responsible for his or her own actions and, thus, as a site of legal imputation for obligations and rights. Subsequently, when this biological division was transferred from the body of the individual to that of humanity, the process of depersonalization was driven to the point of no return. Sucked back into its purely corporeal substratum, the biospiritual core that the modern tradition had called person was now deprived of all its attributes, in favor of collective entities – national, ethnic or racial in character – whose fates were predestined by indissoluble blood ties. The personal subject was left no space for autonomy to make individual choices, let alone to form free relations with other people – an activity now turned into a deadly struggle for survival. In the early decades of the 1900s, the most influential human sciences – sociology, anthropology, linguistics – discovered a deadly point of encounter with zoology through a redefinition of human nature that overlapped (or underlapped) onto that of the animal. Instead of being the ancestral origin of the human genus, the animal ended up becoming the internal threshold and parameter for measuring degrees of humanity – or lack of humanity – arbitrarily assigned to human types, which were divided and juxtaposed on the basis of their supposed racial quality.

When the defeat of Nazism began to be apparent, it was quite natural that the very concept of person that had already been battered by nineteenth-century biopolitics and then finally gutted by Nazi thanatopolitics would reappear at the heart of the philosophical, ethical, and legal reconstruction of the democratic culture. Since Nazism, by identifying the human directly with the body, had taken away any ability for human beings to transcend their corporeal matter, it seemed that the first thing to do was to give them back their decision-making power. Human beings were once again endowed with a rational will in relation to themselves and their fellows and made masters of their own fate within a framework of shared values. This is exactly what the concept of person promised, now that it had returned strongly to the fore, along with a whole range of meanings it had acquired in different cultural contexts. This need for renewal was also greater than the difference of principle between the secular view and the Christian view, in the sense that in both cases what mattered was to restore responsibility to humans – before God, themselves, and others. Not surprisingly, the first, and perhaps the most influential definition of the concept – by Jacques Maritain, who had a leading role in drafting the 1948 Declaration – centered on this need for self-determination:

the human person possesses rights because of the very fact that it is a person, a whole, master of itself and of its acts, and which consequently is not merely a means to an end, but an end, an end which must be treated as such. The dignity of the human person? The expression means nothing if it does not signify that by virtue of natural law, the human person has the right to be respected, is the subject of rights, and possesses rights.[7]

Maritain's definition should be understood in all its programmatic significance. The intrinsic connection between person and human rights lies precisely in the self-determination that a human being – every human being, regardless of race, social condition, or gender – can and must exercise in its own regard. This claim is not inconsistent, if kept within rational limits, with the right that God has over humans in the Christian conception (which Maritain shared). It actually follows from it, since humans receive their sovereign right over themselves and over everything belonging to them from divine sovereignty. When conceived of in the vocabulary of the person, then, "the notion of right is even more profound than that of moral obligation, for God has sovereign right over creatures and He has no moral obligation towards them (although He owes it to Himself to give them that which is required by their nature)."[8]

<h1 style="text-align:center">4</h1>

Is this appeal to the notion of person all that is needed to reactivate the blocked dynamic of human rights? Does it suffice to make human beings the natural subject of law, and law the irrevocable attribute of human beings? Even a quick glance at the contemporary scene makes it clear that the answer is no. If we look at the 60 years that separate us from the Declaration of 1948, we certainly cannot argue that fundamental rights have been extended to all human beings, or even that there has been a significant reduction in the number of people who remain uncertain that their vital needs will be satisfied. Despite the rising rhetoric of humanitarian commitment, human life remains largely outside the protection of the law; so much so that one could easily argue that, even in the context of an increasing juridification of society, no right is more disregarded than the right to life for millions of human beings who are condemned to certain death from starvation, disease, and war. How is this outcome possible in a situation where the human being is thought of as a person? As I argue, this outcome occurs *because* of the conceptual lexicon of the person, not in spite of it. My thesis is that the dispositif of the person, intended by the creators of the Declaration on Human Rights to fill in the chasm between man and citizen left gaping since 1789, produced an equally profound gap between rights and life. The very paradigm that appears to be a vehicle for their epochal reunion acts instead as a separation filter, or as a differential diaphragm between two elements that fail to meet up, except in the form of their separation. To understand the underlying reasons for this effect, we must become aware of the fact that what we have here is not a lexical innovation: this is a formal construct that has been around for a very long time and has assumed different forms from one time to another, depending on the context in which it was deployed. From this deeper perspective, the very logic of citizenship, with the exclusion it establishes toward those who lack it, can be considered an internal structure of the ancient and very effective mechanism of splitting, or doubling, which finds its primary expression in the idea of person.

To grasp its distinctive traits, we must trace the concept back to its original source, itself split between a theological matrix and a legal one.[9] Instead of trying to identify which came first, or which is more relevant, it makes more sense to examine the effect that each created on the other over time. Siegmund Schlossmann, in his classic essay on *Persona und prosōpon im Recht und im christlichen Dogma*,[10] attributed the structurally antinomic character of the idea of person to its hybrid descent, simultaneously Christian and Roman. It refers both to mask and to face: image and substance, fiction and reality. Moreover, personhood came into being precisely at the point of transition – and divergence – from the first to the second. Originally understood as a stage garment or theatrical costume, *persona* also began to designate the individual who wore it. The character played by the actor constituted the intermediate segment between the two meanings: it was through the interpretation of a role, by molding an individual, that, little by little, the mask was imprinted on the face of the wearer, until they corresponded in every detail. As Adriano Prosperi observes in his masterful study on this topic,[11] a further stage of integration between representation and reality can be traced to the death masks of wax that were molded directly on the face of the deceased, thus corresponding perfectly to the facial features. What could better convey the sense of total adhesion between the fictional person and the real person (even if dead)? The death mask was no longer what hid or altered the true face of the individual it covered: rather, the true face was revealed in its definitive expression. In other words, in the face of death it was no longer the human being who donned a mask, but the mask that was incarnated in the human body, to the point of constituting its most authentic expression.

This ritual, reported by Suetonius, transposed into the Christian liturgy the ancient custom of wearing the mask of an ancestor on solemn occasions; yet it also affords us a glimpse of the gap that separated the person and the body precisely at the moment when it united them. More than representing the human being in its bodily dimension, the death mask actually had the role of representing its spiritual dimension, or moral quality, from the perspective of an afterlife. This transition, clearly informed by theology, intersected with the Aristotelian distinction between the three souls – vegetative, animal and rational – only the last one of which referred to the idea of person. Regardless of whether the Christian or the Aristotelian influence predominated, the person, or personality, while adhering to the human being like a mask to the face of the deceased, was in any case reserved to its spiritual part, and was therefore separate from, or even opposed to its corporeal part. The doctrine of the Trinity, superimposing three people onto one God, both reflected and reinforced this growing spiritualization of the concept: projected onto the divinity, the attribute of personhood came back to the human being, scored in a metaphysical key that distanced it more and more from its biological substrate.[12] The Christian tradition was thus able to be reunited with the Neoplatonic one, which viewed the soul as a prisoner of the body, the same way in which the person, implanted into the living matter of the individual, was projected irreducibly outside it. From this perspective, the same distance that originally separated the mask from the face was reinstated: not as the difference between fiction and reality now, but as a distinction, in the human being, between an individual dimension with a moral, rational character and an impersonal dimension with an animal nature. Boethius's definition of person as "an individual substance of a rational nature" (*naturae rationalis individua substantia*: in *De persona et duabus naturis*, chapter 3) established the clearly decorporealized meaning of this term. Both the Cartesian tradition – with the prior distinction between *res extensa* and *res cogitans* – and the Lockean tradition, which assigned a functional rather than substantial character to personal identity, are inscribed within this division: in both cases, 'person' qualifies that which, in a human being, is other than and beyond body. Far from identifying the living being in its entirety, inside of which it is nonetheless inscribed, person corresponds rather to the irreducible difference that separates the living being from itself.

## 5

The Roman legal tradition not only failed to bridge this gap; it transferred it from the unique sphere of the individual to the entire fabric of human relations. Human beings were united – in the generality of the law – exactly by what divided them. Or, if you prefer, they were divided by the form that connected them in a common destiny. The essence of the idea of person can be explained precisely in terms of this complex dialectic of unity and separation, inclusion and exclusion. It was the most general category within which all the others were arranged through a play of consecutive bifurcations that led from genus to species, without ever stopping, however, at a particular human being. Thus, from the "most important division in the law of persons" (*summa divisio de iure personarum*), according to which people were distinguished initially either as slaves or as free men, stemmed the division between those who were *ingenui*, born free, and the *liberti*, those who had been freed by their masters. What stands out about this is the fact that, through the formal filter of the person, the law continued to maintain a distance from the concrete existence and corporeal density of an individual human being, focusing instead on the development of abstract categories: *servi, filii in potestate, uxores in matrimonio, mulieres in manu, liberi in mancipio*, but also *addicti, nexi*, and *auctorati* were all classes of human beings who were *alieni iuris* – that is, subordinate in various ways to an external form of mastery that made them objects rather than subjects of the law – defined precisely by their *status*, which, from case to case, allowed them to be legitimately killed, sold, used, or even freed by the *paterfamilias* – the only type of living being who was *sui iuris* ['of his own law, autonomous'].

Right from the beginning, then, the role of the law was recognized to be one of defining breaks between categories on a continuum punctuated and regulated according to successive thresholds of inclusion and exclusion. But what the unparalleled creative power of Roman jurisprudence focused on was not so much the definition of various statutes as the semantic vacillation created on their borders, sometimes with disruptive effects on the very provisions that governed their relations. The most notorious example of this zone of indistinguishability, or overlapping between statutes, was certainly the slave, who was eternally suspended between the condition of person and that of thing. The slave was a thing with the role of person and a person reduced to the status of thing, depending on whether we look at the actual functions performed in Roman society or at the strictly legal classification. A slave was literally a non-person within the more general category of person: a living thing, or life walled up in a thing. In the way they were used or treated, slaves were assimilated to other property, or to animals owned by the master: likened to a speaking tool versus a dumb one, a slave was therefore entirely under the control of its owner, both with regard to his/her actions and with regard to his/her body. In some cases a slave could legally represent the absent *dominus*, or even act as the administrator of a *peculium* [private property or small savings]. Similarly, although deprived of any legal personality, a slave could still be subject to legal punishment, on condition that it be particularly cruel and ignominious, or could even testify before a judge, under torture. Anyone who killed a slave – other than the master, who was always entitled to do so – would be convicted of murder (as when a person had been caused to die) or would be required to provide monetary compensation to the owner (as in the loss of any other asset) according to the master's preference.

But the most distinctive locus of this ambivalence, because it was encoded in a strict, often performative ritual – "I affirm that this man [a slave] is mine by Quiritary right (*hunc ego hominem ex iure Quiritium meum esse aio*)" recites the formula for claiming

ownership of a slave (*vindicatio in servitutem*) handed down by
Gaius (*Institutions*, 4. 16) – lies in the transition from one state
to the other, from slavery to freedom and vice versa. The effect of
personalization, or depersonalization, that resulted from this ritual
is important; but what really matters are the countless intermediate stages marking the transition between person and thing, which
was never entirely completed and always reversible. The figure
that most vividly expressed this extraordinary inventiveness of the
Roman legal experience was manumission – *manumissio*: the
freeing of a slave. This procedure could take three different forms:
a ritual performed before a magistrate and involving a rod or staff
called a *vindicta* (*manumissio vindicta*); dispositions in a will
(*manumissio testamento*); or registration in the census (*manumissio censu*). However, manumission always depended on the sovereign will of the owner. In the first form, emancipation was a
consequence of the fact that the legal claim (*vindicatio in liberta-
tem*) brought by the *adsertor libertatis* (the advocate for the slave's
freedom, a role played by someone in agreement with the *dominus*)
was not opposed by a *contravindicatio* from the master. In the
second form, the one by means of a will, emancipation only
became effective upon the death of the master, when the obligations that continued to bind the *libertus* to the owner in the other
cases were consequently extinguished. In the third type, *manumissio* took the form of the *dominus* registering the slave in the census
lists, eventually allowing him or her to be recorded in the rostrum
of free citizens. But what characterized the procedure of manumission in all its forms was its incompleteness; the distance, in other
words, that remained from the actual condition of freedom, as
measured by precisely defined degrees. Once put into motion,
emancipation could depend on a subsequent event taking place;
pending its occurrence, the process remained suspended. In the
meantime, a slave who was still considered as such but was close
to freedom was defined as *statuliber*. The lex Junia Norbana (AD
19), intended to regulate the whole matter, made a distinction
between independence acquired in this way and Roman citizenship, which was granted to very few compared to all the others
who were instead given the same status as the *Latini* from the
colonies. Since the *Latini* were permitted to trade but not to make
a will, it has been rightly observed that they lived like free men,

but went back to being slaves when they died. The institution specifically designed for its depersonalizing effects was codified under the name of *diminutio capitis*, and it was futher qualified as *minima*, *media*, and *maxima* according to the degree of reification it accomplished. Freedom – only if desired by the master – was in these ways limited in form, extent, and duration. This reflects the fact that it was intended not as an originary condition, but as a derivative one, which human beings could attain to only temporarily and occasionally, through an artificial process of personification. Ultimately, freedom was nothing but a "remnant" or residue – a narrow, fragile projection – off the natural horizon of slavery. No human being was a person by nature – not as such. Certainly not the slave, but not the free man either: before he became *pater*, that is, a legal subject, he still had to pass through the status of *filius in potestate*, which reflected the fact that, in the changeable dispositif of the person, since human beings arrived into life from the world of things, they could always be thrust back into it.

The condition of children in the Roman family has been discussed at length in the literature, leading to inconsistent conclusions. One school, represented mainly by Pietro Bonfante,[13] has tended to assimilate the status of children to that of slaves. This was opposed by another school, which tends to see a greater difference between the father's power over children and the power exerted over other people *in mancipio*. However, this distinction, which is intended to relativize the absolute nature of the *patria potestas*, in the end brings into relief its great significance for the entire Roman legal system. *Patria potestas* has been aptly placed in the category of sovereignty, not only because of the immense rights involved – starting with the power of life and death (*ius vitae ac necis*) – but also, and perhaps most importantly, on the basis of its duration and essential intransmissibility. This aspect had the greatest effect on the personal status of the *filius*, and thus on the process of the child's continuous depersonalization. As always happens in Roman law, a definitive outcome was never reached: depersonalization changed in response to the continuously varying relationship between general rule and exception. Thus in the classical period the father's power to put his children to death was limited, by comparison to the brutality of the archaic period, by prohibiting the killing of male children under 3 years of age and the eldest daughter. Unless – here is the exception that folds the general rule back on itself – the male children were deformed or the daughter was an adulteress. But even children who could not be killed immediately could be exposed (in other words, abandoned) or sold. In this case, too, although a son might be thrust into a condition entirely comparable to that of the slave, he did not fall under the sphere of *potestas* of the new *pater*, but this was only because he remained under that of his biological father. The *patria potestas* could be extinguished in the form of emancipation only if the son was sold three times in a row, as described by the formula recorded in the Twelve Tables: "If a father sell a son three times, let the son be free from the father (*Si pater ter filium duuit, filius a patre liber esto*)." Only then, after being sold as a thing three times, did the *filius* temporarily go back to being a person before taking on the similarly depersonalizing status of an *adoptio*. What is noteworthy about this is not only the fact that in every 'passage' toward personhood there emerged a new and perpetually changing form of depersonalization, but also the almost inextinguishable character of paternal sovereignty: its superiority, based on blood ties, prevailed even over the buyer's right of ownership, demonstrating that biopolitical submission to the parent was more complete and persisted longer than that of any other object later acquired through purchase. If a slave was fully equivalent to a thing, then the personal condition of a son (meaning, every male Roman citizen) ranged between the standing of a free man and a depersonalized condition more debased than that of a thing.

## 6

The functional separation between human beings and rights that characterized the Roman dispositif of the person was reproduced, though a series of variations, throughout the entire course of the modern legal system, making deep incursions into our time. Of course one can insist, as many historians do, on the discontinuous stretches that unquestionably cut this path into separate segments, starting from the confine that, according to conventional wisdom, separates the law of the 'ancients' from that of the 'moderns.' This is fine, as long as we do not lose sight of the underlying conceptual framework that connects at a deep level seemingly very different terminological formulations. The jurists of the ancient system always preserved a keen sense of this continuity, almost as if they were aware of the impossibility of standing outside that extraordinary and terrifying machine of social discipline that was Roman law as a whole. The power of abstraction and separation that its formalism held must have appeared equally inescapable to them.[14] Certainly, the foundational distinction between human as a natural entity and person as an artificial category – one created by the law, around which a whole complex world of relationships and differences, powers and dependencies was gradually being articulated – could hardly have escaped their notice. Riccardo Orestano has reconstructed this conceptual node, one that unites the semantically and categorically distant ancients and moderns on the same horizon of meaning.[15] If, in the mid-sixteenth century, Hugues Doneau (Donellus, 1517–91) noted that "a slave is a man, not a person; man is a term of nature, person is a term of civil law" (*servus homo est, non persona, homo naturae, persona iuris civilis vocabulum*), Hermann Woehl (Vulteius, 1565–1634) later limited personhood to "a man possessing civil status, as it exists in the tribe, in personal freedom, in citizenship, and in the household" (*homo habens caput civile, quod positum est in tribus, in libertate, in civitate, in familia*). Finally, Arnold Vinnen (Vinnius, 1588–1657) brought the distinction to completion when he argued that "a man is anyone for whom a human mind connects with a human body" (*homo dicitur cuicumque contingit in corpore humano mens humana*), whereas "a person is a man with a certain status, just as if he had been clothed in it" (*persona est homo statu quodam veluti indutus*). Not only is *homo* – the word generally reserved in Latin for a slave – not a *persona*; the word *persona* is the *terminus technicus* that separates the juridical capacity from the naturalness of the human being.

This tradition, distinguished by its exceptional systematic rigor, began at a certain point to appear alongside, or even to oppose, another line of interpretation, one that had less doctrinal certainty and tended to unite aspects that the first school kept strictly separate. First appearing in the late Christian period and developed with some theoretical sophistication in medieval scholasticism, it found its most consistent application in the work of the natural law jurists. After a few more lexical shifts, it joined course with seventeenth- and eighteenth-century German Pandectism. The most obvious transformation concerned a shift from an objectivist conception of the law, typical of the Roman approach, to a subjectivist one. In the latter approach, rather than being plugged into an objective web of legal relations, the individual was increasingly understood as a subject with certain naturally inherent privileges. While in classical and medieval Latin, and at least until Descartes, the term *subiectum* in reality meant the object of what, by then, was some form of external control – subjection to a complex of objective rules and regulations – Hobbes first, and then Leibniz overturned this ancient meaning, making it the subject of a sentient, functional activity. At this point the distance between *persona* and *homo* was so small that it practically disappeared. The moment all human beings were considered to be bearers of a rational will, regardless of differences in status or social standing, they were for this very reason also considered to possess a legal personality. In this way, instead of rights being superordinate to the subject, they become the subject's defining trait, understood as the power any subject has over itself and the things that belong to it. From this point of view, the difference between *homo* and *persona* that the Romans upheld no longer had a reason to exist. When the French Revolution went on to sanction the equality of all people, the era of human rights was finally able to gain a foothold, later to be definitively consecrated in our time.

However, it would be misguided to believe that the mystery – the false foundation originally contained in the term 'person,' at once face and mask, whole and part, actor and role – has been solved. The moment the person ceased to be a general category into which someone could be transferred, passing in and out of it the way they did in Rome, and became a quality implicit in every human being, it revealed itself to be different and superimposed on the natural substrate it was implanted in. And this all the more as – or to the extent to which – it was identified with the rational and volitional or moral part of the individual, the part invested with a universal value, so to speak. This is exactly how that splitting, or doubling, that first separated the human being as a simple *homo* from the general category was re-established within every individual.[16] It might be said that the rights claimed for the legal personality have as their object its selfsame subject, and that they are consequently the most contradictory expression of the logical *dispositif* that assigns to the subject the property – and therefore the objectification – of itself. But this is exactly how the dualism that was supposed to be overcome ended up being reintroduced, only in an even more powerful form. Far from disappearing, the splitting action penetrated from the outside inside, dividing the human being into two areas: a biological body and a site of legal imputation, the first being subjected to the discretionary control of the second. Once again, and perhaps even more than before, the person is not the same as the human being in its entirety. The person is actually superimposed onto the human being – but also juxtaposed with it – as an artificial product of the very law that defines it as such. Following this line of reasoning, Hans Kelsen may well argue that person and human being are different concepts, despite the modern expression or declaration of their identity (as is indeed apparent from the technical distinction between legal person and physical person). Contrary to those who would like to view the legal person as somehow partaking in reality, Kelsen denies any reality-based attributes to the physical person as well. He refuses to interpret the latter as anything but the mythological personification of the rights and obligations related to human behavior: "The so-called physical person, then, is not a human being, but the personified unity of the legal norms that obligate or authorize one and the same human being."[17] Once again, and with increasing clarity, the *dispositif* of the person appears to be an artificial screen that separates human beings from their rights, a confirmation that something like 'human rights' is impossible.

## 7

We have already seen how the juridical category of person intersects at several points with the political category of sovereignty.

In the works of Thomas Hobbes, the two terms are wound up so tightly in a conceptual tangle that one is made the effect of the other. The notion of person is what introduces and defines that of the sovereign state: "This is more than consent, or concord; it is a real unity of them all, in one and the same person."[18] Chapter 17 of *Leviathan*, where this quotation appears (a chapter entitled "Of the Causes, Generation, and Definition of a Commonwealth"), starts with an examination of the Greek and Latin terms, further evidence of the long and persistent influence of the classical legal tradition. It also gives an idea of just how much change the vocabulary of this tradition has undergone, and, to an even greater extent, its semantics. Although the term is used in a variety of registers in Hobbes's works, the most novel aspect relates to the way he transfers the Roman separation between *homo* and *persona* to the concept of person itself, now separated into natural and artificial:

> A person, is he, whose words or actions are considered, either as his own, or as representing the words or actions of another man, or of any other thing, to whom they are attributed, whether truly or by fiction. When they are considered as his own, then he is called a *natural person*: and when they are considered as representing the words and actions of another, then is he a *feigned* or *artificial person*.[19]

Hence, as we already know, not only does the person not coincide with the natural being in which it is located – otherwise it would not even be able to represent itself – it can also represent another human being. Further on, pushing his deconstruction of personal identity to even greater depths, Hobbes goes on to argue that even inanimate things like a church, a hospital, or a bridge can be "personated." While the traditional view differentiated between the functions of person and of human being, it had never put into question their primary relationship. The break with the classical tradition could not be starker: it is as if Hobbes had skewed the perspective in the dialectic described earlier between mask and face, image and substance, fiction and reality entirely toward the first term. Not only does the mask not have to adhere necessarily to the face of the wearer, it can also cover the face of another entity. If truth be told, this is the case that most interests Hobbes: so much so that it could well be said that the artificial person does not follow logically from the natural person, but the other way around. This is also because the representation of someone else is more directly evident than the representation of oneself. But the underlying motivation for the logical and semantic prevalence of the artificial person over the natural one lies in the fact that its definition is precisely what enables Hobbes to construct his own theory of sovereignty, which will serve as the cornerstone of his entire system. Given that the sovereign does not have to represent himself, not only is he an artificial person, he is also the person who represents all the other persons. To put it more precisely, he is the only agent of personalization, since, strictly speaking, before the sovereign is constituted nobody can define him- or herself as person, whether artificial or natural, because in a state of nature everyone coincides with his or her living (and, before long, dying) being. In other words, there is no such thing as the transcendence of self, which is the necessary condition of personality. As for the other 'feigned' persons, attributed to non-human entities, "such things cannot be personated, before there be some state of civil government."[20]

But if the sovereign is the agent of personalization, he is at the same time and for this very reason also the principle of depersonalization: what he removes from the other persons is what the very core of their personality resides in. To grasp the full significance of this double-crossover effect, we must start from the relation between author and actor inherent in the idea of artificial person. The actor is the one who represents the actions or words of another, namely the author. Put in terms of political theory, in the state of the *Leviathan* this distinction is evident in the sovereign, the actor par excellence, in whom all the authors – united in the covenant that constitutes him – recognize them-selves to the point of considering all the actions he performs as their own creations. This is the reason why none of the contract-ing parties can ever complain about a sovereign command – even when it is to their detriment or actually condemns them to death – since every command was previously authorized by them. Already in this instance, in the transfer of their power, but also of their ability to challenge any abuse of that power, we begin to make out the reifying nature of the sovereign personalization. It certainly creates juridical subjects, giving them a personality that they did not have in the state of nature – but in the form of utter subjugation: rather than (and before) being subjects *of*, they are constitutionally subject *to* an actor who, in interpreting their role, strips them of any decision-making capacity. This out-and-out exchange of subjectivity has been rightly connected to a lexical discontinuity in the category of authority between the original Latin version and the Hobbesian variation.[21] The Roman *auctor* – derived from *augere* – is the one who takes the initiative in an act and perfects it both in public law (the *patres auctores*) and in private law (someone's guardian), as well as in criminal law (the author of an offense). However, rather than using the verb *to authorize* (enable another to speak in one's name), Hobbes transfers the right, ownership, and corresponding power entirely into the hands of the actor. In this way the actor becomes in turn the exclusive subject of what he says or does, making himself entirely autonomous from the control of the authors who initially set him in place and, in so doing, also forfeited their capacity to intervene in his actions: "The author, or legislator is supposed in every commonwealth to be evident, because he is the sovereign, who having been constituted by the consent of every one, is supposed by every one to be sufficiently known."[22] Furthermore, the sovereign, defined once and for all as the authorized actor, turns out to be the effective author of all his own acts; but, as befits an author, he can also create other actors – the "public ministers"[23] – who will in turn transform themselves into authors with respect to the subjects who are placed under their authority.

The effects hardly stop here, though. We have already seen how, once the sovereign-actor is established, he becomes the sole author of the law. As we have also seen, he further has the ability to make things, or inanimate entities, into new legal persons. But, in addition to transforming things into persons, by his very nature as a collective person that includes all others he also has the ability to thrust people into the realm of things. What, we might ask, really remains of the person – understood as the autonomous site of judgment and will – after the 'authors' have conferred "all their power and strength upon one man, or upon one assembly of men, that may reduce all their wills, by plurality of voices, unto one will," and they have submitted "their wills, every one to his will, and their judgments, to his judgment"?[24] Moreover, persons who take on this status upon their entrance into the civil order only enter into relationship with the person who legitimately represents them. Because of this, they forfeit their capacity to represent anyone else and, more importantly, even to represent themselves. They thus lose their personal status at the precise moment they acquire it. The fact that the person is constrained to obey the sovereign outwardly, in the external sphere of his or her actions, but not inwardly, in the internal sphere of his or her conscience and judgment, which remained free, splits the person into two different parts, which later would be reproduced in the irreconcilable modern dichotomy between human being and citizen. Separated from everyone else by the vertical thread that binds him or her, individually, to the sovereign, each person is splayed apart from its own inside in such a way that the two are impossible to reunite. This is the double effect – of personalization and depersonalization – that sovereignty has on the body of the person: it makes the person something that no longer has body, and the body something that can no longer be a person.

## 8

Let us regain our perspective by retracing the broad outlines of the picture we have filled in thus far. The renewed emphasis on the category of person that began in the 1940s arose from the need to counter the Nazi political ideology, or political biology, focused on the absolute primacy of the racial body and on its ensuing depersonalization. In opposition to the idea – or, more accurately, the practice – of crushing the subject into its own biological substance, the perfectly understandable reaction of the democratic culture that emerged victorious from the Second World War was to restore some distance between the rational or spiritual element of human beings and their mere corporeal given. From this point of view, the opposition of principle between the secular and the Catholic perspectives remained secondary to – or at least appeared to be reconcilable from the perspective of – the much more marked difference that irremediably divided them both from the thanatopolitics of Nazism. The absolute immanence of the 'spirit of the race' with respect to the individual or collective body in which it inhered was countered by the transcendence (or at least transcendentality) of the personal subject with respect to its biological being. The essence of the person was seen to lie in this irreducible difference that distinguishes each of us by our mode of being; in other words, in the non-coincidence of the being and its mode. While according to what we have called biopolitics – which Nazism both fulfilled and perverted – the human being is nothing but its biological being, the person is defined as that core of rational will that is implanted by God or nature into the individual body, but cannot be identified with it. On these lines, and according to the canonical formulation, the person is substance *and* relationship, a relationship between two substances – divine and human, spiritual and bodily, subjective and objective – that overlap without ever becoming completely blurred.

But assuming that this is true, what form does this relation take? How are we to define the relationship between the two entities, or principles, that constitute the person? This question – fueled simultaneously by legal, ethical, and political issues – stands at the center of a debate that has yet to be exhausted today. Its terms also trace out an unexpected stretch of contiguity, on the conceptual plane, between seemingly distant, or even opposing ideas. To begin with, the definition of Maritain that we discussed earlier already calls into question the category of sovereignty: a person is the entity that is qualified by its dominion over its own biological substrate, a whole that can unify and dominate its parts. What is striking about this definition is the intensely political characterization Maritain lends to the originally legal problem of human rights; so much so that he derives the priority of rights over obligations, by analogy, from a comparison with the absolute power the Creator holds over his creatures. But even more significant in terms of the essential 'duplicity' of the category of person is the way he classifies as 'animal' the other part of the self over which the person exercises his or her dominion: "if a sound political conception depends above all on concentrating on the human person, it must at the same time bear in mind that this person is an animal gifted with reason, and that the part of animality in such a set-up is immense."[25] We need to focus on the foundational bond that exists between the two terms of the relationship: each of the terms is necessary for the other to be identified by contrast with it. A human being is a person precisely because (and only if) it maintains full control over its animal nature. And the reason why human beings have an animal nature is so they can measure against it their sovereign status as a person.

At this point it is difficult to ignore a certain connection with the opposition between the relational and the vegetative lives, which Bichat placed at the origin of the biopolitical line of thought that first deconstructed and then wiped out the idea of person. Except that, while in that scenario – and increasingly along the thanatopolitical drift we reconstructed in the first chapter – the vegetative part prevailed over the relational part both in intensity and in duration, the relationship is now reversed in favor of the rational volitional part, which is destined to rule over the animal. In both paradigms an animal part is disclosed within the human: the human harbors the animal inside it. But now, according to a conception that can be traced back both to Catholicism and to the Enlightenment, the human being is such – a person, that is – if it is in the position to control the animal, to dominate its animal life. This is the case, adds Maritain, both in the individual body and the body social; it, too, is divided along a line that separates the healthy area, governed by reason and morality, from another area, which is unhealthy and irrational, governed by instinct and destructive passion. Nazism, in his view, did nothing but unleash this animal dimension against the personal one, in a form that we must now reverse into its opposite. Humans (the individual human being and humanity as a whole) must once again leash up their animal, the brute animality that forms the dark background out of which the human person comes to light. This attitude avoids both the utopian assumption that the animal part does not exist – in other words, that man is fully human – and the risk of becoming its slave:

> It appears that a political philosophy based on reality must struggle against two opposite errors: on the one hand against an optimistic pseudo-idealism that extends from Rousseau to Lenin, that feeds

men with false hopes, and that, while pretending to hasten it, distorts the emancipation to which they aspire; and, on the other hand, against a pessimistic pseudo-realism that extends from Machiavelli to Hitler and that bends man under violence, returning only the animality which enslaves him.[26]

## 9

The remarkable semantic proximity that these expressions create between Maritain's 'personalism' and the 'animalism' of the biopolitical vision – which this 'personalism' is intended to counteract – should come as no surprise. From a hermeneutic perspective with a deeper view into the past – one that is able to perceive the deep geological strata beneath the surface cracks in which they open up – it is clear that both develop from the same enduring element, namely the Aristotelian definition of man as the rational animal. As Heidegger also observed (with a different intention and in a different context),[27] once this premise has been assumed, there are only two perspectives to choose from, and they are ultimately mirror-images of each other. Either there is a tendency for human life to be absorbed into animal life, as it was claimed in nineteenth-century biophilosophy, along a course brought to its ultimate end by Nazism; or an asymmetrical relationship is established between them that submits the animal part to the unconditional dominion of the other, on the basis of its preliminary characterization as rational and volitional. From this genealogical or, better still, archaeological point of view, one can similarly say that even the personalist tradition that sought to oppose biopolitics wound up being caught in its violent mechanisms, or that the ancient dynasty of the person annexed to its system of meaning even the biopolitical apparatus that was intended to undermine it.

On the other hand, when compared over a long period of time, if the democratic conception, with its universalist formalism, is incompatible in principle with the deformalization of biopolitics, the same cannot be said for liberalism, which came out as the real winner in the epochal double battle against Nazism and communism. As Foucault has shown[28] – using an interpretive framework that is far more productive than the tired old dichotomy between totalitarianism and liberal democracy[29] – the liberal perspective (distinct in its turn from the democratic one), although seemingly opposed to the biopolitical view, actually constitutes a particular cross-section of it. In no way, of course, must we blur the clear boundary that separates the bio-thanatopolitics of the Nazi State from the individual biopolitics of the liberal type, which represents its clear reversal.[30] While the first is based on an increasingly totalized restriction of freedom, the second is devoted to the progressive expansion of freedom. But it does remain bound to the same imperative, which is to manage life productively: in the first case, to benefit the racial body of the chosen people; and in the second, to benefit the body of the individual subject who becomes its master. In spite of this fundamentally important difference, what makes these perspectives overlap or intersect through a somewhat similar conceptual vocabulary is the animalization or reification of one area of the human over another, which is simultaneously opposed to it and superimposed on it. For liberal culture – unlike Nazism – the dividing line between animal and human passes through the individual, and not through a racial hierarchy of peoples. The fact remains, however – actually it becomes even more evident – that the reasoning behind the relationship thus established between body and thing is in any case analogous: if you start from an instrumental conception of life – whether enlisted in the service of the sovereign state or of the individual – the condition of one tends to slide into that of the other. Now, contrary to what has been assumed, making the definition of human rights dependent on the language of the person has not managed to stop this drift. And the reason why it has been unsuccessful, as we have shown by opening up a wider perspective on the issue, is that what created this drift is the very language of the person itself. To the extent that this language identifies, inside the human, an extracorporeal core defined in terms of will and reason, it necessarily ends up thrusting the body into an animal or vegetal dimension, putting it in direct contact with the sphere of things.

As we have seen in Maritain, the category through which we reached this outcome is sovereignty in itself. But it was soon flanked, and then covered, by the category of property, in a typically more liberal key: in a tradition that dates back to John Locke and John Stuart Mill, a person is such – a human being takes on personhood, in other words – when it has ownership of itself. While, for Locke, "every man has a property in his own person: this no body has any right to but himself,"[31] for Mill, "the only part of the conduct of any one, for which he is amenable to society, is that which concerns others. In the part which merely concerns himself, his independence is, of right, absolute. Over himself, over his own body and mind, the individual is sovereign."[32] Even in this case, the body – over which the person exercises his or her proprietary dominion – is thought of as thing, as a bodily thing or a reified body. Therefore in each individual the *dispositif* of the person works at the same time toward personalization (in the rational part) and toward depersonalization (in the animal or bodily part). In short, only a non-person, living matter with no personhood, can give rise to something like a person as the object of its own subject. Just as, conversely, a person is a person if it reduces to thingness that out of which it arises on the basis of its own rational–spiritual status. This process of depersonalizing the body – opposite and complementary to the biopolitical process of corporealizing the person – is common even to manifestly different conceptions, such as the Catholic and liberal, whose visions are formulated by using the categorial language of the person, and hence, necessarily, also by using the language of the thing, since not only can one not exist without the other, but it is precisely the case that one engenders the other. Remarkably, in the current debate on bioethics, this point of intersection, which connects to a single conceptual premise ideological camps that seem to be deployed along opposing fronts, has failed to be noticed. Both those who advocate access to their body – to improve it, to manage it, to modify it, or even to rent it out, to sell it, or to euthanize it – and those who declare it off limits because it is the intangible property of God, the state, or nature, must first posit its conversion into a thing. Only because it has been placed beforehand under the category of *res extra commercium* ['non-tradeable things'] can human life be declared sacred by Catholics and qualifiable by others. Otherwise, if this were not the case, if the body were not already reified, the question of whose property it was would not even come under discussion: the body itself would be a subject (obviously, an impersonal one) of self-determination.

## 10

According to the classic doctrine of civil law, the human body is juridically impossible to mix up with a thing. The starting point of this distinction remains the Roman *summa divisio* ['main partition'] into *personae* and *res*: only things can be the property of persons. Now, being the inseparable substrate of the person, the body cannot belong to anyone. It cannot belong to others, but it cannot belong to the subject either: it coincides with it in the dimension of being but not in the dimension of having – in other words the body is not something we have, it is what we are. For this reason, as Ulpian expresses it (*Digest* 9.2.13), "no one is to be regarded as the owner of his own limbs" (*dominus membrorum suorum nemo videtur*). And yet, because of the way it defines them, the same legal system that separates between body and thing also opens up several passageways between these two spheres, first of all by recognizing the existence of entities that, while they are not things, are not classified as persons either. Just think of the uncertain status of embryos, gametes, and ova; or of that of aborted fetuses, which are considered equivalent to clinical waste – not to mention corpses.[33] The complex legal problems arising from their definition offer the clearest evidence for the vacillating ontological status imposed on these entities by their very nature. Should someone who steals an embryo be charged with theft, as if they were appropriating a thing belonging to someone else, or with kidnapping, as if they were abducting a person? And what, exactly, is the crime of desecrating a corpse: an attack on the person that the corpse was at one time, or on the thing he/she/it has become? When, exactly, is a body declared to be a corpse and a fetus a person? What was it before and what will it be after its finite segment of life as a person? Could we say that this being with personhood emerges from and returns to a state of thingness? Or that what precedes and follows being a person is never a simple thing, but perhaps a not-yet-person or a no-longer-person, located halfway on the route from thing to person and from person to thing?

But this first set of problems is accompanied by another, no less fraught with irresolvable aporiae. If the body as a whole is legally distinct from the thing, to the extent that it can never be owned as property even by the subject who inhabits it, does this also apply to its individual parts? For some of these parts – such as excrement, secretions, nails, teeth, and hair – once separated from the body, their inclusion in the category of *res derelictae* ['things thrown away'] or *nullius* ['nobody's'] is not in question. But for medically amputated organs or tissues the discussion is more complex. Who owns an appendix or a kidney after it has been removed: the surgeon, whoever takes possession of it, or the patient? This apparently insignificant question has given rise to legal disputes that in some cases have gone to trial – such as when a medical team sold to a pharmaceutical company a gallbladder taken from a patient with an extremely rare blood condition, to be used for the manufacture of certain drugs. Even leaving aside the verdict – which was delivered by a Court of California in favor of the patient and against the hospital, subsequently forced to compensate him – the 'philosophical' issue at stake was precisely the status of the organ and thus, through it, that of the entire human body of which it was a part. Whether its property – because this is ultimately what was at issue – was assigned to the patient, to the doctors, or to the corporation in question has no effect on the fundamental ontological choice of referring to a bodily part as a thing that can be owned as a piece of property. Once this premise has been assumed and established through a court sentence, it is bound to be valid for all other similar cases: if all the bodily parts of a person belong to him or her, then the body as a whole must surely belong to the person as well.[34] But, if so – if the body is legally ascribable to the realm of things from which classical civil law theoretically distinguished it – then the legitimate owner can dispose of it just as for any other piece of property or slave: "Everyone is the owner of themselves," argues Bertrand Lemennicier in this regard.

> This legal concept, which consists in asserting ownership over one's own body, is consistent. The human body is an object like any other

whose owner is perfectly identified. This notion can be universalized: every human being, whether potential or not, every spirit incorporated into a biological machine either does not benefit from property rights over this machine because it is the occupant, or it does possess them.[35]

Specifically in order to defend this ownership against anybody who may wish to attack it, subsequent laws have made the sale of organs from a body, whether alive or dead, conditional upon the explicit consent of the party involved, prohibiting all forms of remuneration. But this has implicitly reinforced the reification of the body, even if without the courage to take this idea to its logical conclusion: the removed organ is a thing because, unlike a person, it can be donated; but it is not a thing because, unlike any other object, it cannot be sold.

The other shifting threshold that marks both the boundary line and the passage between the realm of living beings and the realm of things that can be owned as property is the institution of the patent.[36] It is common knowledge that artificial inventions can be patented; but not so natural products – a category that includes life in all its human, animal, and vegetal forms. Just as one cannot take possession of *res communes*, including the air, rivers, and mountains, one cannot patent something that is already available in nature. However, in this instance as well, as has already happened in the realm of transplanted organs, the logic of the market on the one hand and biotechnology on the other have radically altered the previous legal protocols, while the law continually revises the boundaries between what is natural and what is artificial (or, as we have phrased it, between non-thing and thing). In the short space of a few decades – from the Plant Patent Act of 1930 to the most recent court decisions – the patenting of the first modified plant seeds was permitted; this was followed by the patenting of modified single-celled microorganisms, then of transgenic animals – thus coming closer and closer to human nature itself. Now, what concerns us in conceptual terms beyond the issues pertaining to each of these cases is on the one hand the overall direction they delineate, from the natural to the artificial – in other words the gradual reification of life; and, on the other hand, the characteristic pattern this process takes, which is always the transfer of a given product from one category into another, through an opening and redefinition of their ontological boundaries. So what was considered vegetal was at some point assimilated to the mineral, what was once considered animal was assimilated to the vegetal, until a zone liminal to the human was reduced to the animal. In this way the boundaries that protected the various genera from a legal point of view, by virtue of the presupposed difference between these genera – boundaries first created, then dismantled by the law – were passed over. The general transition of humankind toward thingness, which has become the predominant tendency of our time, was opened up by this continuous transition from human to animal, from animal to vegetal, and from vegetal to mineral. Neither the difference between animate and inanimate beings nor the difference between natural and artificial have withstood the allied pressure of economy and technology. This new zone of indistinguishability both belies and plays out the consequences of the ancient Roman *divisio*. As long as the identity of the person is derived negatively from the thing – from its not-being a thing – the thing is destined to become the continually expanding space of everything the person distinguishes and distances itself from.

## 11

The ancient Roman connection between personhood and the reification of the body is at the heart of liberal bioethics. Of course, to bring this into focus, we must train our gaze to see things crosswise, behind the obvious discontinuity between 'ancients' and 'moderns' – to perceive within the objectivism of the former and the subjectivism of the latter a metaphysical node, bound to a formalism that was conceived (as it was by the Romans) in order to define abstract relationships, and an intensely biopolitical procedural mode that was designed to destroy any mediation between law and biological life. This node, as we have repeatedly said, is defined by the dispositif of the person. While it, too, has undergone the semantic twists and reversals described earlier, its essential function remains the assumed separation, operated inside the human being, between a natural, merely biological, corporeal element and another element, which is transcendental and construed from time to time as the site of legal, rational, and moral imputation. Now the argumentative strategy of the branch of contemporary bioethics that defines itself as liberal – in contrast to the Catholic branch[37] – consists in continually broadening this original difference, codified by the Romans, between *homo* and *persona*: not all human beings can aspire to qualify as persons; but, equally, not all persons are human beings. Both Hugo Engelhardt and Peter Singer, considered the greatest exponents of this school of thought, insist on both these principles; the two thinkers are linked together by the ontological distance between personal life and biological life, which they both take for granted. With the failure of the idea of body as an inseparable substrate of personhood, this latter becomes (or is re-established as) a qualifying condition dependent on a series of attributes – reason, will, moral sense – that not all human beings possess, or that they possess only partially. It is precisely the presence, or the extent, of these "indicators of humanhood," as Singer describes them, that divides what we commonly call human beings into two distinct categories: those who can be considered simple 'members of the species *Homo sapiens*' and those who deserve to be called real and proper 'persons.'[38]

Of course, between the two categories, taken in their typological purity – simple *zoe* on the one hand, *bios* endowed with maximum value on the other – lies a series of intermediate degrees, which go from one to the other according to increasing or decreasing thresholds of personality that depend on the point of observation. In any case, whether you start from the beginning or from the end of life, what really qualifies as 'person' only occupies the central section: that of adult, healthy individuals. Before and after this lies the no man's land of the non-person (the fetus), the quasi-person (the infant), the semi-person (the elderly, no longer mentally or physically able), the no-longer-person (the patient in a vegetative state), and, finally, the anti-person (the fool, whom Singer puts in the same relation to the intelligent human being as obtains between the animal and the normal human being – albeit with a clear preference for the animal). To this categorization of the different classes of living beings, which we might characterize as 'static,' he then adds a dynamic one, defined by the transition from one status to another. This is especially the case with what Engelhardt calls a 'potential person,' namely someone who, although intended to land in the world of persons – at least until they are expelled from it as a result of old age or of some incurable disease – is still *alieni iuris* ['of another's right'] and therefore *in potestate* ['under the dominion'] of its parents. The reference to Roman law, and in particular to the two 'transitional' figures between person and thing – *manumissio* and *mancipatio* – catches the eye not only in relation to the overall framework defined in these terms, but also in relation to specific references, such as this quotation from Gaius: "As Gaius remarks in his *Institutes*, 'if we capture a wild animal, a bird or a fish, what we so capture becomes ours forthwith and is held to remain ours so long as it is kept in our control.'"[39] If this is true for animals that are captured and enslaved, it also holds for a newborn child or for a parent who is no longer mentally or physically able to regain his or her health: these are subjected to the absolute power of adult family members, who exercise over them a guardianship not far off from the 'hand' of the ancient *paterfamilias*. The healthy adult relatives can keep them alive and provide care for them, or they can hand them back to death on the basis of precise medical and financial calculations: "At present parents can choose to keep or destroy their disabled offspring only if the disability happens to be detected during pregnancy. There is no logical basis for restricting parents' choice to these particular disabilities."[40] Moreover, if we are to remain within the Roman legal experience, we may recall that fathers of deformed or monstrous children were exempted from the prohibition of killing any of their children who were younger than three. When the relationship between the presumed quality of his or her life and the cost of his or her care is judged to be uneconomical, the family members themselves can decide to end the life of an elderly person who is irreversibly ill and thus now outside the bounds of personhood, or that of a defective child who has yet to enter inside these confines:

> Newborn babies cannot see themselves as beings who might or might not have a future, and so cannot have a desire to continue

living. For the same reason, if a right to life must be based on the
capacity to want to go on living or on the ability to see oneself as
a continuing mental subject, a newborn baby cannot have a right
to life.[41]

Expressing the views of a cultural front whose membership is
anything but meager, these texts evacuate the meaning out of the
notion of human rights in a manner that is only too obvious, by
revealing its constitutive antinomy. But what turns out to be even
more significant is the decisive role that the 'deciding' machine
of the person plays in this evacuation. The person is what legally
separates life from itself, what makes life the terrain for a preliminary decision about what must live and what may die, because
it is a simple thing in the hands of those who, thanks to their
superior ontological status, are exclusively qualified to dispose of
it. The fact that Singer feels the need to differentiate his version
of 'a life worthy to be lived' from the sadly notorious version
found in the Nazi eugenics manuals[42] is symptomatic of a proximity sensed even by thinkers whose efforts to deny it only serve
to confirm it. The Nazis, too, argued, exactly like these thinkers,
that 'unworthiness' was defined not from the point of view of
society, but from the point of view of those being considered for
elimination, precisely because they are non-persons, sub-persons,
or anti-persons. Although the conscious intentions of liberal bio-
ethicists are entirely remote from those of the Nazi slaughterers
and certainly arise from strict moral protocols, this does not
eliminate an unconscious semantic affinity between them: it is
rooted in a conceptual vector that has been around for a very
long while and is therefore resistant to the shocks and reversals
it has undergone over time. Observed from this standpoint, where
even opposites find an original point of tangency, the formal
abstraction of Roman law seems to topple over into the concrete
immediacy of biopolitical power. When examined along a single
problematic axis – as defined by the dispositif of the person –
lines that at first glance seemed to diverge now come together
again from the side of their opposites: personalization and depersonalization are nothing but different flows of the same
process, one that is ancient in origin but whose effects are far
from being exhausted.

## 12

The thinker who, as early as the 1930s, saw with utter clarity the contradictory outcomes of this implication was Simone Weil. When Weil, with a radicalism that may appear biased, located the origins of Hitlerism in the experience of Rome, she was referring specifically to the performative power of a legal tradition whose aim from the beginning had been to turn people into things:

> It is singularly monstrous that ancient Rome should be praised for having bequeathed to us the notion of rights. If we examine Roman law in its cradle, to see what species it belongs to, we discover that property was defined by the *ius intendi ed abutendi*. And in fact the things which the property owner had the right to use or abuse at will were for the most part human beings.[43]

In contrast with the dominant view, then, and in direct polemics with Maritain's thesis on the primacy of rights over obligations, Weil sharply denounced the sovereign relationship between rights and personhood:

> The notion of rights, by its very mediocrity, leads on naturally to that of the person, for rights are related to personal things. They are on that level. It is much worse still if the word 'personal' is added to the word 'rights,' thus implying the rights of the personality to what is called full expression.[44]

The reason she gives for this rejection is the dual dependence of the person on society and of rights on force. As regards the first, its necessity derives from the natural tendency of the person to seek protection for its prerogatives in a social order that inevitably ends up oppressing it. As for the other relation of implication, the one between rights and force, this arises from applying the same measure to different situations and to subjects endowed with different powers. When this happens – in actuality, almost always – the only thing that guarantees or imposes an inevitably iniquitous sharing is force:

> The notion of rights is linked with the notion of sharing out, of exchange, of measured quantity. It has a commercial flavour,

essentially evocative of legal claims and arguments. Rights are always asserted in a tone of contention; and when this tone is adopted, it must rely on force in the background, or else it will be laughed at.[45]

Looked at from this perspective, what appeared to be two different impulses toward self-negation – of the person in the interest of the collectivity, and of rights with regard to force – now appear as complementary sides of a single immunitary current aimed at the preservation of a privilege threatened by those who are excluded from it. What Weil grasps by connecting it to the root of the exclusionary dispositif of the person is the character of the 'right' – particularistic per se, at once private and privative. A right, to make sense, to distinguish itself from a mere fact, can only protect a certain category of people, leaving out all those who do not fall within its scope. Once assumed as an attribute or predicate of subjects rendered such by possessing specific social, political, and racial characteristics, a right ends up coinciding with the dividing line that separates and opposes them to those who are deprived of it. To imagine that the same privileges could be extended to everyone, concludes Weil, is ridiculous: "the claim is both absurd and base; absurd because privilege is, by definition, inequality; base, because it is not worth claiming."[46]

This is how far she goes in deconstructing a paradigm that, despite the changes in its lexical register, has locked the whole of Western civilization into an orbit marked by the principle of discrimination. Weil does not limit herself to this – to raising the rhetorical curtain behind which lies hidden the dreadful rhetorical dispositif of the person: she initiates a potentially alternative discursive vector. If the category of person has provided a flow channel for a continuous power of separation and subordination between human beings, the only way to evade this coercion lies in reversing it into the mode of the *impersonal*: "What is sacred, far from being the person, is what, in a human being, is impersonal in him. Everything which is impersonal in man is sacred, and nothing else,"[47] because only from and through the impersonal can justice be sought, which Weil radically distinguishes from rights. Just as rights belong to the person, justice pertains to the impersonal, the anonymous – that which, not having a name, stands before or after the personal subject, without ever being identical with it and its supposed metaphysical, ethical, and juridical attributes. To understand the meaning of this enigmatic expression better, Weil offers an immediately graspable example: if a child gets an addition wrong, the mistake arises out of its person. If the calculation is right, it means there is no person, and the child adheres to the impersonal order of things:

> Perfection is impersonal. Our personality is the part of us which belongs to error and sin. The whole effort of the mystic has always been to become such that there is no part left in his soul to say 'I.' But the part of the soul which says 'We' is infinitely more dangerous.[48]

The stress belongs in the second part of this sentence. The part of the person that should be rejected is precisely the one that says 'I' or 'we'; better still, the logical thread that ties individual self-consciousness to collective consciousness in the grammatical mode of the first person. In contrast, the impersonal is what prevents this transition, what preserves the singular pronoun by protecting it from the simultaneously self-protective and self-destructive slide into the general. This means that Weil does not establish a purely contrastive relationship between the person and the impersonal. The impersonal is not simply the opposite of the person – its direct negation – but something that, being *of* the person or *in* the person, stops the immune mechanism that introduces the 'I' into the simultaneously inclusive and exclusive circle of the 'we.' It is a point, or layer, which prevents the natural transition from the splitting of the individual – what we call self-consciousness or self-affirmation – to the collective doubling, to social recognition.

What this may be, this way of being beyond or on the other side of the first person, Weil fails to explain. Or at least she places it in a semantic horizon she defines as mystic – not a convenient object of direct analysis to be conducted at the time.[49] The most important thing about the notion of the impersonal is the connection that begins to emerge with the notion of the singular, seemingly opposite to it. Only by defusing the dispositif of the person will human beings finally be able to be thought of as such – for what they have that is most unique, but also for what they most have in common with each other: "Every man who has once touched the level of the impersonal is charged with a responsibility towards all human beings; to safeguard, not their persons, but whatever frail potentialities are hidden within them for passing over to the impersonal."[50] The need Weil evokes is that of severing the constitutive connection between rights and personal property, of overturning the particularism of the legal form into the consciously aporetic figure of 'common rights,' those that belong to everyone and no one. This is what lies behind the intention of re-establishing – against personalism – the primacy of obligations over rights: the obligation of each, added to that of all the others, corresponds in a global count to the rights of the entire human community. Only the community – conceived of in its most radical signification – can rebuild the connection between rights and human beings that was severed by the ancient blade of the person. But how can it, in the impersonal mode, without losing the singular element that is still implicit in the idea of a person? How can it neutralize its exclusionary power, at the same time safeguarding the relational impulse that makes the person something different from the isolated individual? Does such a thing as a non-personal person exist, or a non-person in the person? Without being able to provide an exhaustive response to this question – the very question that led to the writing of this book – the next chapter will present a series of moments, or movements, of thought in which it has been formulated at one time or another, always in varying ways.

# 3

# Third Person

---

## 1  Non-Person

In a well-known article whose possible implications have yet to be fathomed, the great French linguist Émile Benveniste drew a clear distinction between the first two personal pronouns and the third. Despite the superficial symmetry that appears to unite them into a single paradigm made of three terms, the pronoun *he/she* is radically different from *I* and *you*. This is so much the case that the third person can actually be defined by its opposition to the first two: not only is *he/she* not what *I* and *you* are; it is what they are *not*. In other words, rather than being their reverse, it is something irreducible to the indissoluble dyad they form. To understand this fundamental dissimilarity, we have to start from the characteristics that bind the first two persons to the same bipolar type. First, they have an exclusively discursive dimension. Instead of referring to an external reality, to an objective given of any sort, they take on meaning only within the act of speech in which they are uttered: "*I* signifies 'the person who is uttering the present instance of the discourse containing *I*.'"[1] This leads to the other specific quality that distinguishes the first and second person, namely their unicity: both the *I* who is speaking and the *you* who is listening are unique to their respective instance of discourse. Their only validity lies in reference to themselves and to the spatial–temporal context implicit in the utterance. This feature unites them to a series of other pronominal or adverbial 'indicators' such as *this*, *here*, and *now*, which refer to the present time of the discourse situation. Even if the *I* refers to another time or another space, it always talks to the *you* in the present; it cannot escape the contemporaneity that defines its momentary condition as speaker. By speaking, by pronouncing oneself to be *I*, one is literally 'presented': both to oneself and to the other who takes part in the conversation. But the aspect that most profoundly qualifies the first and second persons – in contrast to the third – is their mutual reversibility. The fact that they have a purely linguistic reality, precisely because they never refer to an external object, makes them empty signs, to be filled in by the speakers in turns. Since anyone who pronounces the word *I* assumes the role of subject in relation to the *you*, he or she is destined to be replaced as soon as the *you* takes the floor in its turn, thereby placing the previous speaker in the silent role of listener.

Benveniste stresses the specular symmetry that unites the first two pronominal pronouns. Against any theory aimed at elucidating their dissimilarity or independence, he points to their absolute complementarity. It is true that the *I*, by always referring to itself, places the other, whom it calls *you*, at a distance. But this is exactly what the *you* does, the instant it takes over the role of speaker previously occupied by the *I* in the discursive instance. This means that, rather than marking a dissimilarity or a contraposition, this distance constitutes the very locus in which the two terms mutually imply each other. Just as the *I* always, directly or indirectly, implies a *you* whom it addresses, similarly there is no *you* without an *I* who, by separating the *you* from itself, designates it as such. This does not mean that the first two persons are on the same plane: the *I* is always the one who defines the field of relevance, as well as the spatial and temporal coordinates within which something like a *you* can come into being. The *you*, from this point of view, presupposes the *I*. It is its *alter ego* – other, but in relation to the *ego* who declares it to be such by splitting itself, or doubling itself, in its *own* alterity. As much as the *I* may want to respect the *you* in its independence, preserving it in its transcendence, the *I* cannot help but exert an effect of mastery over it, since that alterity is logically dependent on the definition of the

*I* itself. Indeed, what defines alterity, if not a point of contrast with respect to an entity that precedes it? Despite all the rhetoric about the surplus or excess of the other, when the two terms are compared, the *you* is conceivable only and always in relation to the *I*. It can never be anything but *non-I* – its reverse and its shadow. Following this line of reasoning, Jacques Lacan takes the discussion into a different sphere – not entirely unrelated to the strictly linguistic one – in a seminar given the same year as the publication of Benveniste's essay, when he observes that "the support of this *you*, whatever form it takes in my experience, is an *ego*, the ego expressing it. [...] The *I* who says, *I am the one who am*, this *I*, absolutely alone, is the one who radically sustains the *thou* in his interpellation."[2] But, as soon as the logical and semantic primacy of the *I* is suggested, the symmetry with the situation of the *you* is re-established, once again on the plane of language, by the continuous exchange carried out by the first two persons. As we have seen, what continuously passes back and forth between them is the role of subject. Since only one can occupy it – the one who calls itself *I* – the subjectivization of the first term automatically desubjectifies the second, until such time as it acquires subjectivity in its turn by desubjectivizing the first.

The third person escapes a dialectic of this sort, in a form that not only differentiates it from the first two but also opens up a completely different horizon of meaning. What is put into play with the third person is no longer a relationship based on exchange between a 'subjective person,' indicated by the *I*, and a 'non-subjective person,' represented by the *you*, but the possibility of a non-personal person, or more radically, of a non-person. Its extraneity to the dialectic between *I* and *you* also makes it extraneous to the logical mode of the person: "The consequence must be formulated clearly," observes Benveniste regarding the verbal person. "The 'third person' is not a 'person'; it is really the verbal form whose function is to express the *non-person*."[3] This is the point of the entire article; and, even at the risk of overstating himself, Benveniste cannot stress it enough:

> The 'third person' must not, therefore, be imagined as a person suited to depersonalization. There is no apheresis of the person; it is exactly the non-person, which possesses as its sign the absence

of that which specifically qualifies the 'I' and the 'you.' Because it does not imply any person, it can take any subject whatsoever or no subject, and this subject, expressed or not, is never posited as a 'person.'[4]

Benveniste's argument is that the third person is not limited to weakening or modifying the distinguishing traits of the other two persons; rather, it reverses them into their opposite by pushing them into a space outside their own formulation. Just as the person – in the alternating form of the *I* and the *you* – can only refer to itself in a purely discursive situation, similarly the third person – the non-person – always refers to an objective type of external referent. It refers to something, or even to someone, but to a someone who is not recognizable as *this* specific person, either because it does not refer to anyone at all or because it can be extended to everyone. One might say that it is situated precisely at the point of intersection between no one and anyone: either it is not a person at all, or it is every person. In reality, it is both at the same time.

In order to demonstrate the non-personal character of the third person, Benveniste offers a wide range of examples drawn from the Indo-European languages, which show with increasing clarity the structural distance between the first two pronouns and the third. For the Arab grammarians in particular, if the first person is 'he who speaks' and the second is 'he who is spoken to,' the third is 'he who is absent.' While, as we have seen, the scope of the meaning of the *I* and *you* is an eternal presence – doubled in the representation that one term creates of the other – the scope of the meaning of the third person is absence. The third-person verb conjugations of many languages also lack an ending, a marker, or a prefix: what is absent is always the subjective quality of the person or, better perhaps, the personal identity of the subject. Not surprisingly, the third person is the only one that can be used to predicate a thing. This does not mean that it cannot refer to a human entity; however, the difference lies in the fact that this entity does not have the self-reflective form of the person. This point is fully elucidated in the case of the impersonal, where the verb includes the subject of the action, or even annuls it. In these cases, in expressions like *huei, tonat, it rains*, the process is seen as something objective, occurring without any connection to an agent; it is viewed rather as an event without a subject, or without constituting a subject: "Hence," Benveniste argues, "*volat avis* does not mean 'the bird flies', but rather 'it flies, (scil.) the bird.' The form *volat* would be enough in itself and, although it is nonpersonal, includes the grammatical notion of subject."[5] By way of further confirmation, Benveniste notes that in several languages the form of the third person pronoun (like the term *ella* in Italian) is used allocutively – addressing an interlocutor who is present – seemingly for opposite purposes, but in actuality with the same intention: namely to take the normal status of personhood away by placing the interlocutor above it, out of reverence, or below it, out of contempt. Once again, the third person evades the personal mode that binds the first and second persons to the same linguistic fate.

All this does not just make the third person the most unusual of persons – specifically because it escapes the inevitable mirroring experienced by the first two; it is also the highest degree plural – and indeed the only true plural. Benveniste concludes his analysis by noting that the first- and second-person plurals – the *we* and *you* – are not really plural at all. They are an expansion, respectively, of the *I* and *you*. They are not a pluralization, since a *unicum* cannot multiply itself; rather they are an extension in the form of a collective person, broader and weightier than the *I* and the *you*, but with the same identity-related connotations.

> It is clear, in effect, that the oneness and the subjectivity inherent in 'I' contradict the possibility of a pluralization. If there cannot be several 'Is' conceived of by an actual 'I' who is speaking, it is because 'we' is not a multiplication of identical objects but a *junction* between 'I' and the 'non-I,' no matter what the content of this 'non-I' may be. This junction forms a new totality which is of a very special type whose components are not equivalent: in 'we' it is always 'I' which predominates since there cannot be 'we' except by starting with 'I,' and thus 'I' dominates the 'non-I' element by means of its transcendent quality. The presence of 'I' is constitutive of 'we.'[6]

The only person that has a plural, even when it is in the singular – or rather, precisely because it is in the singular – is the third. But this is because, strictly speaking, it is a non-person. Its peculiarity, to be more precise, resides in it being neither singular nor plural. Or in being both: singular/plural. It breaks down the traditional opposition, typical of the semantics of the person, between these two modes. By not being a person, by being constitutively impersonal, it is both singular and plural: "This non-person which, extended and unlimited by its expression, expresses an indefinite set of non-personal beings [...] Only the 'third person,' being a non-person, admits of a true plural."[7]

## 2 The Animal

Seeking the essence of the juridical phenomenon during an era that seemed to signal its demise – at the height of the Second World War – Alexandre Kojève located this essence in the intervention of a third person in the binary dialectic between two others. There is *Droit* [law, right] every time an impartial and disinterested third intervenes in the interaction between two human beings, annulling the reaction of the second to the action of the first. Whether the right of the first is considered to be the cause or the effect of the third's intervention – depending on a subjective or objective understanding of the juridical phenomenon thus defined – does not necessarily change the ternary character of its structure. In any case, *Droit* is constitutively bound to the figure of the third. Georg Simmel had already noted this in another context,[8] emphasizing the qualitatively decisive role of three – as compared to all other numbers, larger or smaller – in the creation of a social situation. For a juridical situation to exist as an eminently social situation, there must always be a triad:

> *Droit* is an essentially social phenomenon. *Tres faciunt collegium* [three individuals make a corporation], a Roman adage states, and this is profoundly true. Two human beings are just as little a Society (or a State, or indeed a family) as an isolated being. For there to be a Society, it is not enough that there be an interaction between two beings. It is necessary – and sufficient – that there also be an 'intervention' of a third.[9]

This aspect – the way it differs from a situation with one or two terms – is what makes the juridical phenomenon irreducible, in its essential character, to any other sphere of human experience. Not only to areas that are patently dissimilar to it, such as esthetic practice, or to ones that, conversely, appear to overlap it, such as economic trade, but also to the adjacent territories of morality, religion, and politics. As far as morality or the ethical relation is concerned, it can only erroneously be defined as such, since a moral individual only relates to him- or herself. Even if subject to the judgments of others, moral individuals always measure themselves against their own ideal, on the basis of an inner law that they share with no one else. If morality is thus different from *Droit* because it is essentially monodic, religion is different because it is inevitably dyadic. In contrast to what is believed by someone who considers God to be the supreme judge, and therefore 'third,' in actuality the divine being is always a disputing party in a two-party relationship with the religious believer, who turns to God in expectation of punishment or salvation. As far as political action goes, Kojève makes light work for himself by adopting the well-known ideas of Carl Schmitt (whose model of investigation, moreover, inspired the entire *Phénoménologie*)[10] on the political inconceivability of "a disinterested and therefore neutral third party":[11] since the political experience is inherently characterized by an adversarial relationship between friend and enemy, it is different from, and even contrary to, the juridical experience. That a juridical act involving a political enemy is impossible is all too evident; but this is also the case for an act involving a friend, who cannot be regarded as such by a truly impartial judge. The fact that in normal situations public law appears to be incorporated into the formal structure of the state in no way removes the categorial distance between the two spheres: only when *Droit* is removed from an essentially political situation – meaning, ultimately, one that is conflictual – can it perform its literally neutral action, with no prejudice toward one or the other. Not surprisingly, in Kojève's view, its full unfolding will have to wait until the end of politics, when it can pass from a state of potentiality into one of actuality.

This thesis, whose aporetic consequences we will examine shortly, points to the other area of inquiry – historical and genetic, or, more properly, genealogical in nature – that Kojève pursues in this text. No longer working toward phenomenologically defining the essence of *Droit*, he now devotes his efforts to locating its origin diachronically and tracing its historical development. The very sharp distinctions that he draws in the first part naturally tend to soften or to take on a dialectical form when placed in a unified framework, constructed around the founding moment of human experience – which is defined by him as the "anthropogenic act." Here we meet up again with a theme examined in its various forms throughout this book, now seen from an eccentric point of view with respect to what we examined earlier: that of the specificity of human nature vis-à-vis our animal origins. Kojève's basic thesis, very loosely based on the work of Hegel, is that human beings become fully and effectively human only through opposition to their animal nature, which serves them as an unavoidable support. The animal we have inside and from which we can never fully emancipate ourselves – an animal that can be assimilated, in its irreducibility, to Bichat's organic life – tends to acquire or perform whatever it desires instinctively, starting from its self-preservation. Human beings, however, are distinguished by an originary lack that can never be fulfilled, because what we desire is to be desired by another: to be recognized, that is, as an absolute value by another. To achieve this, we must annul ourselves as the animal *Homo sapiens* – by putting at risk the life that our animal nature would naturally want to preserve, by entering into mortal combat with another individual, who is motivated by the same negative impulse. The result is the well-known Hegelian dialectic between Master and Slave, which in Kojève's original transcription achieves synthesis in the figure of the Citizen, he who recognizes the one from whom he asks to be recognized in turn.

If this, in its essential traits, is the dynamic of humanization, how is it constitutive of the legal form? As we know, Kojève makes the three figures of the Master, the Slave, and the Citizen correspond symmetrically to the three types of justice that follow one another in time, each of which retains and even incorporates dialectically the positive features of the phase that precedes it. This makes equity – the justice of the Citizen – the most mature synthesis between aristocratic equality and bourgeois equivalence. The same deadly Struggle that pits the two figures of Master and

Slave against each other, on the basis of a mutual agreement to fight, requires a level playing field between the two contenders, and therefore a condition that, if not just, is at least not unjust, as a formal prelude to the realization of the future justice. But beyond this somewhat macaronic outline (marked by its excessive and yet flawed adherence to the Hegelian model), the element that defines the most intrinsic juncture between the dynamics of humanization and the genesis of the juridical phenomenon lies precisely in that process of de-animalization, and consequent personalization, that presides over the constitution of the subject of law. The legal subject takes on its specificity – in a way that resonates strongly with what we examined in the previous chapter – precisely in its detachment from the generic human being that the author defined as the animal *Homo sapiens*:

> The real or actual opposition, created by the Struggle and Work between Man and Nature in general, and the nature or animal in Man in particular, allows Man to oppose the human entity that he calls 'subject of droit' to the animal which serves him as [material] support, and of which it [the human entity] is the 'substantialized' negation.[12]

Unlike many thinkers today, Kojève is well aware of the restrictive and exclusionary use the law has made of the formal distinction between subject of law and human being as such: namely of the biological thresholds – established, or shifted from one time to the next, on the basis of age, gender, physical and mental health, or race – by means of which the dispositif of the law has deployed its prescriptive and selective power. But the fact remains, as Kojève sees it, that there is an objective gap separating the juridical person (in all its possible meanings of 'physical person,' 'moral person,' 'collective person') from the animal support in which it is rooted but which it also rises out from: "The real and actual opposition between man and the animal in man justifies the notion of 'subject of *Droit*' in general, and that of 'moral person' in particular."[13] This is so much the case that the destiny of justice, its progressive development into its most mature, resolved forms, is linked to this opposition, to maintaining and deepening it. Only if the law becomes more and more 'human' – in other words less and less influenced by the original biological ground – will its confines be expanded to include a growing number of individuals. Only when freed from the animal compulsion for survival will law restore to life its most authentically human dimension.

However, bringing to the surface an assumption implicit from the outset in his eccentric Hegelianism, Kojève suddenly turns his argument in a different direction, leading it towards an outcome that radically reverses his earlier conclusions. This takes place in his description of the Universal and Homogeneous State (or Empire), which, at the 'end of history' – namely in the era to come, when history will fulfill all its promises, thus exhausting itself as such – will also bring the juridical dialectic to completion. The fact that the law achieves its own fulfillment only in the Universal State (even if only in the forms barely sketched out by Kojève) was envisaged from the outset, in the different status of the Third. Although the Third is active in all previous stages in the roles of legislator, judge, and police, only in the final state is the Third actually disinterested, because the features of class or nationality that qualified it (and still qualify it in all societies, past and present) will be lost. In other words, while in the legal systems that have existed thus far the third person has never been "anyone at all," except "inside of a given group at a given moment of its historical existence,"[14] in a society that "implies all of humanity," and in which therefore no one has a private interest that has not already been resolved in the common good, the Third may really be "anyone at all,"[15] interchangeable with any other. In this event, when the universal can be reconciled with the individual and essence with existence, the law of persons will be realized, and at the same time will be brought to its end, by true justice: "Justice will be fully realized in and by *Droit* because all human existence will be determined by Justice."[16]

Even more surprising (or disturbing, depending on your point of view) is the fact that, in a note to his great commentary on Hegel, Kojève claims that the Universal State not only leads to the exhaustion of the negating action that produces history, it also marks at the same time the end of the human condition – understood as detachment from its own animal support – and even its folding over onto itself: "The disappearance of Man at the end of History, therefore, is not a cosmic catastrophe: the natural World remains what it has been from all eternity. And therefore, it is not a biological catastrophe either: Man remains alive as animal in *harmony* with Nature or given Being."[17] This means that, at its apex, the juridical civilization – coinciding with that of human history as a whole – will all of a sudden retrace its steps in reverse, slipping back into the same animal dimension from which it had so laboriously emancipated itself. Kojève's conclusion naturally leaves us somewhat perplexed as to its credibility – not only in our eyes, but in those of its author, who in later texts restated and also reworked it. Without attempting to penetrate this conclusion in all its refractoriness – or, even less, to pin it down to any political position, whether reactionary or revolutionary – what emerges is still a vector of meaning that seems to contradict the abstracting effects of the same dispositif of the juridical person that Kojève apparently referred to in a neutral, even positive manner: at the end of time, when the general will coincide with the singular and the proper with the common, the third person will rediscover, or recognize, its own impersonal substance.

This is also what Simone Weil intended, from a very different perspective, when she traced out an impossible coincidence between law and justice: a law in common, that belongs to no one, because it belongs to one and all. "The citizen," says Kojève, in agreement with her, "will act as a citizen, that is, as *any given* member of the community, or on the basis of he or she being a human being."[18] This is the passage out of which the animal substance makes its reappearance: that mere biological life that becomes increasingly resistant to the all too human attempts to overcome it. Without necessarily wishing to pit different biological species against each other, perhaps Kojève's skeptical, ironic gaze came to rest exactly at the point of their possible conjuncture: on a future horizon that belongs neither to the human order nor to the animal order, but rather to the still hazy silhouette of their crossing.[19] Moreover, the fact that the becoming-animal of the human being is located at the end of history suggests that this is not a pure return to a primitive condition, but the achievement of a state never before experienced: rather than a simple re-animalization of the now humanized human, it is a way of being human that is no longer defined in terms of alterity from our animal origins.

### 3   The Other

The extraneity of the Third from the language of the first two is attested by philosophers of the second person as well – in the various shades of dialogue, empathy, and love that they employ at different times – but viewed negatively. In his *Treatise on the Virtues*, Vladimir Jankélévitch situates the third person in a delocutory position that, although formulated in a different context and with different intentions, has remarkable similarities to Benveniste's description:

> Love leads to the Thou [*Tu*] as respect leads to the You [*Vous*], but justice, for its part, leads neither to the You nor to the Thou, because it has no interlocutors; nobody to talk to, to address itself to, to ask questions of; nobody to interpellate in a pleading interjection, nobody to call in an imperious vocative or an urgent invocation. The person of justice is the *third*: the third person is exactly what we mean, and not the intermediary of the mediation interposed between the two extremes of the me [*moi*] and the you [*toi*].[20]

The third person is not – specifies Jankélévitch – someone or something whose task is to relate two distant partners, to link two elements that have been temporarily separated. The person of justice is not the "third-person discursive" in a dialogic situation; rather it is a point of absolute unrelation, because it is external to the sphere of the interlocutor. From this perspective, and for the same reason noted by Benveniste, in addition to escaping a relationship with others, the third person also escapes, to some extent, even a relationship with itself, with its own status as person. Instead it multiplies itself into such an indefinite number that a sort of general depersonalization results:

> All persons of justice are third persons and persons who are definitively third – which is to say: there is no longer a third person, there is no person at all any more, no matter what their number; the only thing left is some agent, anyone at all or Mr. *So-And-So*, a member of a collective made up of individuals that are all interchangeable: the anonymous, impersonal, and headless 'One' [*On*] takes the place of 'Him/Her' [*Lui*] and no longer occupies any particular position in the scheme of conjugations; this faceless

person, which Buber opposes to the 'Thou' [*Toi*] of dialogue, is the person who is no one, the 'One' [*Il*] who is 'no one' [*oudeis*].[21]

What we have here is someone who, given the degree of anonymity, goes beyond even Kojève's 'anyone' or 'anyone at all,' because it is structurally external to the semantics of subjectivity shared by the *I* and the *you* – by the *you* as the privileged interlocutor of the *I*. Except that what for others constitutes a linguistic or logical specificity becomes a negativity or a loss for Jankélévitch, something that is even literally unthinkable. It could actually be said that the whole purpose of his treatise is to defuse this threat, to neutralize this excess by reabsorbing it into the dialectic of the *I* and the *you*. His point of departure, and really the ultimate vertex against which all other 'virtues' are measured, is love, understood as a direct relation that binds the first to the second person, in an ecstatic form that precludes any distance. In this relationship, instead of speaking to a generic *alter*, the *I* speaks to a unique *you*, which is more intimate than its own self: so intimate and unique that it cannot be summoned in the normal form of the indicative, but only in the direct and sublime form of the vocative, in an invocation or prayer. When this *you* slides from the inter-subjective plane of co-presence onto the neutral and objective plane of definition – thus passing from the incommensurable mode of *parousia* to the determinate form of *ousia*[22] – the second person has already ceased to be such in its entirety: it has already started on its dissolutive journey toward an outcome that will eventually cause it to disintegrate and be dispersed in the anonymity of the third. This entropic process proceeds by splitting and serializing the *you*, whose value is based on its uniqueness and irreplaceability. Even the virtue of respect, placed in an intermediate position between love and justice, although arising out of interlocution, generalizes and extends the dialogue from the singularity of the thou [*Tu*] to the plurality of the you [*Vous*]. The interlocutor does not disappear in this median figure – characterized by reserve, or by a difference in status – but passes from the particularity of the singular person, chosen and loved as such, to the generality of a set, a collectivity, or a multitude: "here the duo makes way for a multi-headed, anonymous relationship,"[23] as Jankélévitch phrases it. So there can be no transformation from respect or from the closest of friendships to the face-to-face immediacy of love. Of course, in some cases a commonality of purpose, solidarity in the midst of danger, or sudden camaraderie may arise between previously distant individuals but there is nothing really comparable to the absolute, penetrating immediacy of love and its ardent, limitless proximity. Just as the 'you' [*Voi*] is not the same as the 'thou' [*tu*], neither is the 'we' [*Noi*], even in the highest form of charity, the same as an 'I' capable of responding directly and exclusively to the call of the other who interpellates it.

But this first downgrading of the second person, due to its multiplication, is accompanied by another one, which is even more uncontrollable because it inevitably leads to a sliding toward the third person, and thus to further degradation. Although still situated in a dialectic involving speaking subjects, this happens when there appears an absence heralding the advent of a more difficult, less urbanized Third, like someone who – instead of limiting him- or herself to opening up or pluralizing the dialogue – threatens to break it down completely through an exteriority that runs directly counter to the intimacy of the face-to-face relation. In this event, when the relationship begins to be turned inside out, the *you* (that *you* who is as vital to the *I* as the *I* is to the *you*) feels "expelled from the brotherly duo, kept on the sidelines of every allocution. Here we have a trio of deaf people whose interlocutors are all strangers to each other and absent to each other."[24] In these circumstances, what is still being declined as a grammatical second person turns out in spiritual terms actually to be a third. Already invested with the lack of meaning that evacuates the third person, it is thrust unwillingly before the Nothing, in which the disfigured face of the Impersonal can at last be glimpsed: "the *you* [*toi*], now something indifferent, cannot be distinguished from the other persons of its conjugation except by its ordinary number. Each concrete person can be transformed into an abstract monad, every unutterable *ipse* into an utterable, generic *ipseity*. The conceptualized second person is just about as personal as the *It* in 'it rains.' "[25] Jankélévitch's defensive strategies against this traumatic event, against the alienating effect of the Impersonal, are manifold. The third person is either negated as such by him or driven out by a system that is so focused on the effusive relationship between the first two that it is rendered completely incapable of introjecting or mastering it in any way. The assumption his analysis begins with, clearly framed in terms of exorcism, is that "an absolutely third person is a monster."[26] As something that negates itself – thus disappearing off the horizon of the personal – what else could it be? It is, simply, not: rather than another person, it is an anti-person. Certainly, Jankélévitch admits, a person may be temporarily absent, but always in relation to its moments of presence, which by their fullness push it into absence; in the same way the line that describes a vertical cut is dependent on the blocks that it separates, or silence is made 'audible' only by the cessation of the sounds that come before and after it, thereby creating and interrupting it.[27] So there can be no such thing as a person who is permanently absent: sooner or later it must reappear, thus coming back into the circle of interlocution. Unless (this is the extreme Jankélévitch goes to in order to negate what he is incapable of conceptualizing) the person is dead, of course. What would a third that was truly outside the loving dialogue of the other two be like, he asks. "Can that which is absent [*un absent*] and excluded from all discourse, whether affectionate, imperative or aggressive, even be said to be absent? More likely, it is dead, if death is the absolute, irreparable, definitive absence, and the suppression of all that has presence, whether actual or virtual."[28]

For Jankélévitch, the person who is no longer such, embodied by an impersonal and abstract justice, bears the unsayable name of the 'Other' [*Autrui*]. This is not the third person, which is still in a relationship, however precarious, with the second and with the first, and hence indirectly or obliquely recoverable within the dialogic scheme: "The Other is a Third that has never been and never will be second."[29] It is not someone, anyone, or anyone at all. Rather, it is everyone – and therefore no one, as Benveniste concluded, following a different line of reasoning. Since *he/she* does not exist for me, for you, or ultimately, says the author, for itself, it simply is not. It is an opening, or the outside, of the personal relationship. It is a relationship without personhood and, at the same time, a person without relationship: it is the unrelated, the irrelative, and the impersonal. Pure *flatus vocis*, Jankélévitch insists. Or worse, it resembles what occurs with undifferentiated altruism, that surreptitious way of being unconcerned with anyone by pretending to be interested in everyone: "Forced to choose between immediately and never again, between here-and-now and nowhere, between someone and everyone, the philosophy of the third person chooses *Nunquam*, *Nusquam*, and *Nemo*, to love the whole world, and therefore to not love anybody."[30] To signify the irremediable extraneity of this entity with respect to any other personal declension, Jankélévitch ends up by defining it as the "fourth person," with the idea of permanently expelling it from the horizon. When you reach the fourth – the pronoun that does not exist – the whole system of virtues crashes to a halt and topples over into pure exteriority: into a system to the *n*th degree, where not only are there no more persons, they are impossible to enumerate, because even the first number has been lost – the *ipse* from which the entire dialectic got its start and from which, ultimately, it had never detached itself.

All genealogies stop here. Beyond the third person, in effect, begins the vast, undifferentiated, gray ocean of innumerable, unnamable, interchangeable Others who submerge all ipseity. Because in this twilight world where all beings are others to each other and where, properly speaking, nobody is 'someone,' no matter who they are, every other is at the same time other than the others and other than itself. The 'I' [*ego*] itself is lost, drowned, reified, altering and alienating all its fellows.[31]

## 4 He/She

The entire work of Emmanuel Levinas is traversed and troubled by the question of the third person. It constitutes both the theoretical apex of his thought and its point of internal crisis, its problem and the limit it strikes up against without ever arriving at a solution. At times the question even threatens to split his work into two blocks of meaning that are not easily reconcilable. Far from attempting to neutralize the third person or to exclude it from the encounter between the *I* and the *you* (as Jankélévitch still does), Levinas recognizes it at the foundation of the *you*, as the angle of perspective or the lateral tear that serves to decentralize both poles, even before redefining their relationship. True, Levinas also views the *I* and the *you* as arranged frontally, in a face-to-face relationship. Indeed, no one sees the *I* as being interpellated, in its absolute singularity, by such a unique and irreplaceable face as he does. But precisely the 'originarity' of the face – the elusive roots of its origin – is what serves to open up a signifying field that is irreducible to the linearity of a relationship between two terms, one that is impossible to transpose into the fixity of a binary form:

> The personal dimension the face of the other imposes on us is beyond Being. *Beyond being is a third person*, which is not definable by the oneself, by ipseity. It is the possibility of this third direction of radical *unrightness* which escapes the bipolar play of immanence and transcendence proper to being, where immanence always wins against transcendence. Through a trace the irreversible past takes on the profile of a 'He.' The beyond from which a face comes is in the third person.[32]

To understand the enigmatic sense – intentionally suspended at the emergence of the 'Enigma' – of these thoughts, we must go back to the criticisms that Levinas directed on several occasions toward the dialectic between *you* and *I*, as it is defined by the philosophy of the second person, and most notably in the version offered by Martin Buber. What Levinas specifically puts into question is the formal (not necessarily personal) character of terms arranged on the same plane, and therefore interchangeable, whether read from left to right or from right to left. This makes one nothing but the reverse projection of the other, alternately one or the other solely on the basis of the position assumed by the first of the terms.[33] What we have here is a topological arrangement reproducing at the philosophical level the implication between the first and the second person established by Benveniste in the linguistic sphere: for Buber, too, the relation between *I* and *you* is also a symmetrical one, of co-presence and reciprocity, which characterizes the position of the two interlocutors in the act of speaking. For the *you* to acquire a subjective role, it must in its turn assume the identity of the *I*: it is the interlocutor of an *I* who has already pronounced itself to be such. Levinas radically reverses each step in this logical and grammatical scheme. It does not suffice to say that the *I* is different from the *you* – that the *you* cannot be assimilated to the *I* – because a formulation of this sort could reduce the alterity of the second person to a simple projection out of a common foundation that preliminarily binds it to the first. In actuality, the second person is completely different from the first, since "language is spoken where community between the terms of the relationship is wanting."[34] The fact that the relationship not only presupposes, but is actually constituted by, the separation of its terms, as Levinas argues, means that the diversity of the other is not to be viewed as a specific difference within a common genus, but rather as an irreconcilable heterogeneity between entirely different spatial and temporal orders. This asymmetry, which is also diachrony, removes the *you* from the logical and syntactic rules of normal linguistic communication, endowing it with an exteriority and superiority with respect to the *I* that Levinas defines as 'mastery.' The subject is interpellated and at the same time expropriated from above – or in any case from outside – this position, in the interest of someone for whom he or she can exercise a form of responsibility akin to the highest form of justice. But the process of alteration that the *I* undergoes, which makes it the object of the *you*'s control, is the same process that has always suspended it to a transcendence so remote that it can only define itself in third person. If the *I*, far from naming itself as such, must decline itself in the accusative mode – "It's me," it says when identifying itself to the other – the *you* in its turn is always uttered in the vocative, as that which cannot be known as an object. The result (but also the presupposition) of this triangulation – in which each term is dominated and at the same time displaced by the precedence of the other – is a kind of curvature of being, which, even in the face-to-face relationship, prohibits the interlocutors from addressing each other by using the informal *you* [*tu*], exposing them instead to the obliquity of a third term most aptly named 'illeity.' Illeity[35] is what opens up the gates of justice, forcing individual action to make an uncompromising commitment to a just responsibility. But what exactly is illeity?

Who is the third person that the 'il' in illeity alludes to? And what kind of justice issues from it? These are the questions – *the* question, as Levinas himself defines it by elevating it above all others – that his entire philosophical inquiry seeks to answer without ever arriving at a definitive response. Because he never does, he also remains trapped in the antinomy continuously created by the varying answers he provides over the course of time, sometimes even in the same work. Taking a cross-section of his entire oeuvre, however, we might say that, throughout the first phase (up to and including the pivotal essays in *Totality and Infinity*), the term illeity is given a predominantly negative meaning. Although it ultimately alludes to the presence of God, Levinas always expresses it in terms of absence, as is implicit in the trace that is crossed out and erased by the ungraspability of that which comes into being only by withdrawing itself. As far as the encounter between *I* and *you* is concerned, although illeity interrupts their dialectic of duality, it does not form a third pole external to them. It is located neither beside them nor between them, but rather at their foundation. Illeity is the non-originary origin toward which both extend without ever being able to reach it; the lateral swerve that deflects their course; the line of separation that distances them from each other, cutting them off even from themselves. It is their *non*-conjuncture, their *non*-reversibility, their *non*-immanence – an excess, margin, or threshold – but never a positive entity, in any case.

This is exactly where the problem lies: if the *il* of 'illeity' can only occur in the negative, only in terms of what it is not and never in terms of what it is; if it is a fault, a void, or a vortex that can never be filled without betraying itself, then how can it ever receive or render justice? That is, assuming that what is meant by justice is not only the precisely directed intention that binds the *I* to the unicity of the *you*, but also a broader relationship, which concerns others as well: not just the other or the Other, but the other of the other, and the other of *each* other. These are the basic terms of the question, the query that at a certain point (or perhaps tacitly from the very beginning) erupts into the philosophy of Levinas with a force of collision that will eventually split it in two, or at least divide it along two parallel axes that are difficult to reconcile.

> If proximity ordered to me only the other alone, there would have not been any problem, in even the most general sense of the term. A question would not have been born, nor consciousness, nor self-consciousness. The responsibility for the other is an immediacy antecedent to questions, it is proximity. It is troubled and becomes a problem when a third party enters.[36]

As early as 1954, in an essay on "The *I* and the Totality,"[37] he embarks on a close examination of his own presuppositions: if radically conceived – in the non-generalizable absoluteness of its terms, that is – the face-to-face relationship would end up excluding all other human beings from the scope of justice except the single chosen interlocutor, and along with it, the very possibility for any true justice. Even though the *he/she* lies at the foundation of the *you* [*Tu*] and therefore is not coextensive with it, the third person remains imprisoned in the unicity of the *you*: it is third only on the horizon opened up by, and relative to, the second. But in this way, if the third is included in the absoluteness of the second, if "the contemporaneousness of the multiple is tied about the diachrony of two,"[38] then the first will never meet up directly with the third, never assume the third in its range of action. Bound by its exclusive commitment to its own other (Levinas describes the close relationship between the two as intimate and 'clandestine'), the *I* is forced to neglect the third. The indifference of the *I* toward the third, toward third parties who have no less right to protection, risks turning into a subtle form of violence.[39]

What the question comes down to in the final analysis is the contiguous, yet oppositional relationship between justice and love. Certainly, love can be considered the original source of justice, but it cannot resolve justice within itself. There is something inside of love – its enclosure in a world of duality – that essentially contradicts justice. Not because love is too pure, but rather – as Levinas writes, reversing the hierarchy that Jankélévitch had established – because it is not pure enough to satisfy the general demand for the good that only justice can provide: "Earthly morality invites us to take the difficult turn leading toward third parties who remain outside of love. Only justice satisfies its need for purity."[40] So, although arising from love, "this definitely does not mean to say that the rigor of justice can't be turned against love understood in terms of responsibility."[41] Naturally, Levinas tends to retain the difference between the poles of love and justice – between the 'interior' third, so to speak, and the 'exterior' third, or, more accurately perhaps, between the exteriority of a twosome versus that of a threesome – thus established within the limits of a logical compatibility. Precisely for this purpose he compresses what he himself presented as absolute anteriority or antecedence into a

synchronic co-presence: the face does not appear first, followed
by the demand for justice, just as charity does not precede the law
but rather underlies and innervates it. When viewed from a trian-
gular perspective, even the most remote past may appear contemporary to what follows it in time. And yet all this fails to alter the
basic conflict: it is not sufficient to expand or vertically extend the
dyadic order in order to obtain a triadic one. The lexicons associated with them are as incompatible as those of the line and the
circle. Nor does it suffice to say, as Levinas does, that justice limits
the absolute ethics of responsibility in the same way in which
responsibility moderates the universality of law. In actuality,
neither can be expressed without contradicting the other: neither
can be brought to fulfillment without at the same time negating
the other. Not surprisingly, the asymmetric adjustment to responsibility that justice gives rise to is what Levinas defines as a *de-
visage*, a disfigurement of the face.[42] This antinomy, still implicit
in *Totality and Infinity*, explodes in all its force in *Otherwise
than Being*:

> The third party is other than the neighbor, but also another neigh-
> bor, and also a neighbor of the other and not simply his fellow.
> What then are the other and the third party for one another? What
> have they done to one another? Which passes before the other?
> The other stands in a relationship with the third party, for whom
> I cannot entirely answer, even if I alone answer, before any ques-
> tion, for my neighbor. The other and the third party, my neighbors,
> contemporaries of one another, put distance between me and the
> other and the third party. 'Peace, peace to the far and the near'
> [Isaiah 57.19], we now understand the point of this apparent
> rhetoric. The third party introduces a contradiction in the saying
> whose signification before the other until then went in one
> direction.[43]

The main point emphasized by the contradiction is the distance
between the principles of unicity and generality, exclusivity and
inclusivity, disproportion and measure: in short, between partial-
ity and equality. Because, if a relationship between two people
necessarily privileges the unicity of the other's *face* that stands
before one, then any form of justice must open onto the plurality
of *faces* that surround it: "Justice is necessary, that is, comparison,

coexistence, contemporaneousness, assembling, order, thematization, the visibility of faces, and thus intentionality and the intellect, and in intentionality and the intellect, the intelligibility of a system, and thence also a copresence on an equal footing[,] as before a court of justice."[44] For the third person to be identifiable – not a third inside the second person, hollowed out or scooped out from its foundation, but rather one that is external even to it, located outside the first and second persons and actually constituted in an absolute outside – in order for this to happen, the dialogical structure of the face-to-face relationship – and thus of the intersubjective dialectic that goes along with it – must be forced open and broken down. The language of the person – or even of persons, as all those evoked by Levinas are – must be turned inside out, into the form of the impersonal. This would lead the verticality of transcendence back onto a plane of immanence and would multiply the singular into the plural. But this is precisely what Levinas cannot do without losing the absoluteness of the *you* [*tu*] – and with it the absoluteness of the *I*, which he always presupposes or makes antecedent to any order of justice, whether broad or narrow, general or specific. The risk of depersonalization in the anonymity of the *il y a* ['there is'] is precisely what his entire philosophical perspective was set up to combat. The neutrality of justice, justice as neutrality – which he also refers to in one of his final essays[45] – does not found a new discourse based on the neutral. It does not inaugurate a crosswise gaze on that 'anyone' or 'anyone at all' in which a truly third person can be reflected on its originary impersonal ground.

## 5   The Neuter

The 'step beyond' that Levinas fails to take is accomplished by Maurice Blanchot. The most striking aspect of this passage is that it does not arise out of a distancing from Levinas, but is inscribed instead within a reversed assumption of his thought, as if Blanchot had chosen to locate his own perspective on the extreme outskirts of Levinas's thought, at the furthest extension of its path, where its semantic boundaries break up and it spills over into its opposite. This makes it difficult to identify, in his many comments on Levinas's work, the line beyond which the most syntonic of observations adopts a critical inflection toward what is, nevertheless, hailed as "a new departure in philosophy."[46] At issue is always the particular relationship that links the *I* and the *you* in the linguistic act, in the form of their separation. How can a relationship exist between terms that are absolute, and therefore unfettered by any relationship? How can such a thing be defined? We know the answer Levinas gave to this question: he identified a third pole lying at the foundation of the *you*, or even beyond it, a pole based on two simultaneously overlapping and diverging modes of justice. While recognizing the power for innovation that this response provides, Blanchot expresses a number of concerns in its regard. They relate to the specifically ethical tone Levinas gives to his own perspective, in explicit contrast with Martin Heidegger's ontology. Can the language of ethics be used to interpret the constitutively aporetic nature of a relationship based on the separation of its terms? But above all, even more pressingly, are they effectively separated if the locus, or means, of this separation is speech, albeit one extended in the infinite difference between the living actuality of 'saying' and the objectivization of 'the said'? True, Levinas dislocates the two parties by placing them at different levels, one infinitely superior to the other, and by conferring on the *you* absolute primacy in relation to the *I*. But apart from the fact that this privilege of the *you* over the *I* is still relative to its position – since a high can only be defined in comparison to a low – spoken language, with the continuous opportunity it provides to clarify, justify, and modify what one has said, in the end restores the symmetry between them that was supposed to be avoided. Not only that, but, while in spoken language the *you* is assumed in its radical alterity, it is also made into an *I* that speaks in the first person at the very moment the *I* addresses its interlocutor, calling it back to its responsibility. In this way this self-referential subjectivity that the discourse sought to evacuate from the beginning is reconstituted, in the intimate presence of speech for whoever utters it.

So what? If this is the final outcome reached by the thinker who dedicated himself more than any other to the deconstruction of the *I–you* relationship, the only remaining recourse is a lateral move – a *pas au-delà* – that is not limited to changing the balance between the two interlocutors, or even the topology of their encounter, but calls into question the dialogic structure itself, in the interest of what Blanchot calls "a relation of the third kind."[47] If a relation of the first kind is to be understood as the dialectical operation that sucks the other into the orbit of the same, and if a relation of the second kind is their unmediated unity in a mode of direct participation, the third kind is a relation constituted by the vertigo that opens up between the two interlocutors, by the interruption that prohibits any reciprocity between them. In this scenario, what is at stake is no longer a difference in status that privileges one over the other, a superiority that suspends the first from the magisterial speech of the second, but a perspectival dislocation of the entire linguistic and logical field, something comparable to the paradigm shift that led from Euclidean to Riemannian geometry. In Riemann's geometry a relation will no longer be described in terms of the number of its terms, since there will no longer be such a thing as a 'term' provided by the subjective prerogative of saying *I* or of speaking in first person. This does not signify merely expanding, or even forcing, the dialogic form to include a third element, as we have seen Levinas do at a certain point. What is under debate, in short, is not the relation between the two yielding to an Other, or even to that entirely indeterminate other referred to as '*autrui*.' If this were the case, if it sufficed to have a third intervene between or beyond the two, it could express itself in subjective terms in its turn; it could also acquire – just like Levinas's 'external' third – the right to speak in the first person. Arguing specifically against a reductive interpretation of this sort, Blanchot reminds us that, "according to certain supercilious grammarians, *autrui* should never be used in the first person. I can approach *autrui*, *autrui* cannot approach me. *Autrui* is thus the Other when the other is not a subject."[48] But what is, who is, and how can we define someone who is unable to assume subjecthood, but who can never be an object either? Someone who is not simply a third added to the first two, but not one of them either? Someone who is not, therefore, one *or* the other but who is *neither* [*né*] one *nor* [*né*] the other? The *terminus technicus* that characterizes this unorthodox entity – alien to logic and to some extent even to grammar itself, external not only to the dialogic relationship but also to the very language it inhabits – is the 'neuter' [*ne-uter*].[49] This is the name – forever excluded, shunned, silenced, or betrayed – that Blanchot gives to an otherness or alterity that is not a person, but is not crushed onto the objective plane of the impersonal either:

> Therefore, and before we delete it, let us keep in mind that *autrui* is a name that is essentially neutral and that, far from relieving us of all responsibility of attending to the neutral, it reminds us that we must, in the presence of the other who comes to us as *autrui*, respond to the depth of strangeness, of inertia, of irregularity and idleness [*désoeuvrement*] to which we open when we seek to receive the speech of the Outside. *Autrui* would be man himself, through whom comes to me what discloses itself neither to the personal power of the Subject nor to the power of impersonal truth.[50]

The reasons for Blanchot's diffidence toward the concept of the 'impersonal' – a concept that he himself uses sometimes – certainly cannot be any residual attachment to the person. On the contrary, when Blanchot writes that "impersonality is not enough to guarantee the anonymous,"[51] his intention is to protect his own perspective from the risk of a dialectical recovery implicit in every internal negative. While the term 'impersonal' remains on the horizon of meaning described by the person, albeit in a purely contrastive or privative fashion, the reference to the neutral opens up a whole new semantic field. This explains the hostility (or at least the lack of comprehension) that the entire philosophical tradition has reserved for it, so that

> one can recognize in the entire history of philosophy an effort either to acclimatize or to domesticate the neuter by substituting for it the law of the impersonal and the reign of the universal, or an effort to challenge it by affirming the ethical primacy of the Self-Subject, the mystical aspiration to the singular Unique.[52]

This refusal, or sublimation, extends even to those who have attempted, in various ways, to tackle the question of the neuter – starting from Freud, who interpreted it in terms of drive and instinct, but from a more anthropological perspective, through Jung, who retrieved it in the form of the archetype, but in a spiritualistic light, and finally to Sartre – who, while including one aspect of it in the notion of the 'practico-inert,' gave it a negative character, marginalizing it to the outskirts of his perspective. What makes the neuter elusive is not any specific feature but, paradoxically, the fact that it does not have any: the way it evades in principle the traditional dichotomies that have marked the history of Western thought, such as being and nothingness, presence and absence, inside and outside. While the neuter does not belong in the sphere of being, this does not make it reducible to nothingness either. Perhaps it can best be described as situated at their point of intersection, where one is ceaselessly rendered into the other: nothingness passing into being, presence emptied by absence, the inside spilling out into the outside. Along these lines Blanchot can well say that the neutral (what he calls this 'word too many'), overflowing from our conceptual lexicon in all directions,[53] "cannot be assigned to any genre whatsoever: the non-general, the non-generic, as well as the non-particular."[54] It is something irreducible to any category, to the extent that, rather than talking *of* the neutral, we should talk *in* the neutral, by which he means a 180-degree rotation of our entire logical and semantic system into a form that corresponds in every way to the transition from the first or second person to the third.

The only thinker who fully grasped this issue was Levinas, starting from his essay on evasion, and especially in his later *Existence and Existents*, when he discussed the notion of the *il y a* precisely in these terms: "the third person pronoun in the impersonal form of a verb [...] designates not the uncertainly known author of the action, but the characteristic of this action itself which somehow has no author."[55] The *il y a* (exactly like Blanchot's neuter), which Levinas sees as situated at the foundation of existence, is an experience in which we lose the distinction between being and nothingness, night and day, life and death: it is a nothingness that continues to be; a day that is swallowed up in the darkness; a death that is prolonged into life. Or even the density of the void, the murmur of silence, the hallucinatory wakefulness of insomnia: not the *I* that keeps watch in the night, but the night that keeps watch inside the *I*, dismissing it from its role as subject, from its identity as person, and from its capacity to be a site of imputation. As an event coming from the outside and directed toward the outside, the plane of the *il y a* is completely external to the personal sphere of consciousness. However, this does not mean that it coincides purely with the unconscious: it is "being as an impersonal field, a field without proprietor or master, where negation, annihilation and nothingness are events like affirmation, creation and subsistence, but impersonal events."[56] This point of maximum coincidence between Blanchot and Levinas is also their maximum point of divergence, almost as if an excess of transcendence, having reached its limit, were to topple over into pure immanence. "It was Jean Wahl," Blanchot remarked about Levinas, "who used to say, in his distinct way, that the greatest transcendence, the transcendence of transcendence, is finally immanence, or the perpetual referral of one to the other. Transcendence within immanence."[57] This crest, this antinomic possibility, is precisely what unites and separates the two thinkers. While Blanchot's concept of the neuter incorporates, and indeed intensifies, all the traits that characterize Levinas's notion of the *il y a*, at the same time it reverses its value. While Levinas sees in its impersonal power the intolerable prison from which we must escape through the formation of the "hypostasis" that the post-Christian tradition has assimilated into the concept of 'person,' Blanchot considers it the very locus of our existence, one that is certainly inhospitable and elusive but to which we are inevitably destined and from which any escape is impossible, for the simple reason that it is always already outside. Indeed it is the outside itself, in its most powerful dimension. Accordingly, not only is thought incapable of neutralizing it – neutralizing the neutral would mean redoubling it, after all; thought must safeguard it as its ultimate possibility.

Before it was contemplated in thought, the neuter was encountered in writing, a form of expression that, unlike the spoken word, finds its ultimate meaning not so much in 'making work' as in disengaging it or 'making it idle' [*disoperarla*], exposing it to its irremediable loss of mastery. Not surprisingly, to write has always meant "to pass from the first to the third person,"[58] that is, to "the unlighted event that occurs when one tells a story."[59] While during the first phase – that of the epic – the third person "becomes the impersonal coherency of a *story*," from Cervantes on it becomes "everyday life without adventure: what happens when nothing is happening."[60] It signals that the writer has relinquished the possibility of saying *I*, delegating this power to the characters, thus destining them to embody a multiple third person, identical to the individual lives of which they are the bearers. At a certain point, at the end of the modern period, a further split at the heart of impersonality was caused by the novelist's withdrawal behind the scenes, represented in an exemplary fashion by Gustave Flaubert, and by the far more devastating decentralization that Franz Kafka performed. With Kafka the absence of a narrative voice, like an irreducible extraneity, penetrated into the subjectivity of the characters, but also into the very structure of the work. This step inaugurated the reign of the neuter in the peculiar mode of the third person:

> What Kafka teaches us – even if this formulation cannot be directly attributed to him – is that storytelling brings the neutral into play. Narration that is governed by the neutral is kept in the custody of the third-person '*il*,' an '*il*' that is neither a third person nor the simple cloak of impersonality. The narrative '*il*' in which the neutral speaks is not content to take the place usually occupied by the subject, whether this latter is a stated or an implied 'I' or the event that occurs in its impersonal signification. The narrative 'he' or 'it' unseats every subject just as it disappropriates all transitive action and all objective possibility.[61]

This implies, or engenders, two cross-effects of the highest importance: first, the aphonia of the narrative voice, cloaked by the anonymous murmur of events; and then the relation of self-nonidentification into which the subjects of the action fall. The movement of depersonalization that in any case erupts like a breach in the compactness of the text is so irremediable that it can be likened to a hole inside another hole through which the words, in flight from themselves, resonate like an empty gong.

This process of depersonalization finds its privileged, although not exclusive, space in writing. Like writing, as we have seen, the task of philosophy is not to think the neutral – since it cannot be objectivized as such – but rather to think *in* the neutral, in other words outside the usual dichotomies of subject/object, being/ nothingness, and transcendence/immanence. Perhaps the most significant symptom of Blanchot's attraction toward a theory of the third person lies in the attempt he made, starting in the late 1950s, to transpose it into political practice. Without being able to account for the complexity and contradictoriness of his political course, even through simplifications, the most striking aspect about it is how he persistently strove to identify a public language corresponding to a philosophy of the impersonal. If you run through all the statements he made and the positions he took, what seems to unite them even more than the arguments he employed from one time to the next is the programmatic erasure of his name – or of any proper name – on behalf of the anonymous and the impersonal. When he writes, in a text opposing De Gaulle's return to power in 1958, that "the power of refusal is accomplished neither by us nor in our name, but from a very poor beginning that belongs first of all to those who cannot speak,"[62] he makes impersonality not only the mode and form of the political act, but also its content. From then on, in all his subsequent efforts, which continued until the 1968 movement in France petered out, he insisted with complete determination on the collective (in other words, the non-personal) character of civic engagement. He confirms this in a letter to Jean-Paul Sartre in December 1960:

> Intellectuals [...] have also experienced – and this is not the least meaningful feature – a way of being together, and I am not thinking of the collective character of the Declaration, but of its impersonal force, the fact that all those who signed it certainly lent it their name, but without invoking their particular truth or their nominal fame. For them, the Declaration represented a certain anonymous community of names, by a remarkable relation that judicial authority precisely endeavors, instinctively, to break.[63]

The final reference to the opposition to the judicial authority should not be limited to this specific episode. It must be placed in the context of a broader critique of the law, advanced in order to support what Blanchot himself will define as a demand, on the part of justice, "for ever greater justice."[64] All the traditional legal categories come under this attack, starting from the founding ones of personal responsibility and personal rights. Along these lines, in a text written for an international review, he will argue that "each person becomes responsible for assertions of which he is not the author, for a search that is not only his; he answers for a knowledge that he does not originally know himself."[65] This is the only way we will arrive at a

> putting in common [*mise en commun*] of literary, philosophical, political and social problems, as they are posed according to the determination of each language and within each national context. This supposes that each person renounce the exclusive rights of both ownership of and intervention in his own problems, recognize that his problems also belong to everyone else, and thus agree to conceive of them in a common perspective.[66]

To what extent this "communism of writing"[67] is difficult, or even clearly impossible, to achieve would be made evident – even more than by the failure of this project – by the direction toward "the disaster" that Blanchot's thought took in later years. The fact remains that few authors have dared to seek a path or to open up a passage as he did – toward a theoretical practice of the third person.

## 6   The Outside

It seems that Michel Foucault was not a person: he was a field of opposing forces, a switch for turning on nameless events, a violent yet gentle movement of extroversion. At least this is the remarkably consistent image of him given by the two philosophers who were closest to him. The first is Blanchot himself:

> I had no personal relations with Michel Foucault. I never met him, except one time, in the courtyard of the Sorbonne, during the events of May '68, perhaps in June or July (but I was later told he wasn't there), when I addressed a few words to him, he himself unaware of who was speaking to him [...]. (Whatever the detractors of May might say, it was a splendid moment, when anyone could speak to anyone else, anonymously, impersonally, welcomed with no other justification than that of being another person.)[68]

Moreover, Blanchot continues, "his first book, which brought him fame, had been given to me when the text was nothing but a practically nameless manuscript" (*encore qu'un manuscrit presque sans nom*).[69]

The second comes from Gilles Deleuze:

> Take Foucault himself: you weren't aware of him as a person exactly. Even in trivial situations, say when he came into a room, it was more like a changed atmosphere, a sort of event, an electric or magnetic field or something. That didn't in the least rule out warmth or make you feel uncomfortable, but it wasn't like a person. It was a set of intensities. It sometimes annoyed him to be like that, or to have that effect. But at the same time all his work fed upon it. The visible is for him mirrorings, scintillations, flashes, lighting effects. Language is a huge 'there is [*il y a*],' in the third person – as opposed to any particular person, that's to say [...].[70]

This figural symmetry – in the lineaments of the impersonal – is not that surprising, since, according to Deleuze, Foucault had grasped the centrality of the third person specifically from his reading of Blanchot's work:

> [A]s in Blanchot: you have to begin by analyzing the third person. One speaks, one sees, one dies. There are still subjects, of course – but they're specks dancing in the dust of the visible and permutations in an anonymous babble. The subject's always something derivative. It comes into being and vanishes in the fabric of what one says, what one sees.[71]

This is borne out by Foucault's theory of statements [*énoncés*], especially as expressed in *The Archaeology of Knowledge*. Just as the conditions of possibility for visibility are found in the being (or, better yet, in the 'there is' or *il y a*) of light, the statement is rooted in the anonymous being of language before any *I* begins to speak. Unlike propositions or sentences, which are associated with a subject endowed with the power to initiate discourse, the statement takes the form of a pure multiplicity, an outflow of singularities, which cannot be derived from an individual or a collective consciousness, or from modifications proper to the same enunciative field. With this, Foucault does not exclude a 'place' for the subject, or a subjective role in each statement or series of statements. Far from denoting an empirical *I* or a transcendental ego, however, this place is always vacant, in that it can be occupied at different times by individuals created by the statement itself, in a mode that is irreducible to the first or second person and congruent only with the impersonality of the third. This means that the statement is analyzed without reference to a cogito: the analysis is not concerned with knowing who is speaking or remaining silent, who is showing or concealing themselves, but rather with the impersonal ground out of which the enunciative function emerges in the form of a 'one says' or 'it is said' [*si dice*]. Rather than a single voice that would necessarily speak through the discourse of each person, we have the set of things said, the differences and connections, the articulations and digressions that may at some point take the place of the subject or receive the name of an author. In any case, " 'anyone who speaks [*n'importe qui parle*],' but what he says is not said from anywhere. It is necessarily caught up in the play of an exteriority."[72] The area that reflects this everted attitude of the statements more than any other is literature.[73] As Blanchot maintained, literature opens up a field of intensity in which the subject is sucked into the statement and, thus, catapulted into its own outside. Unlike the *I think*, which is withdrawn into the interiority of reflection, the *I speak* topples over into an exteriority where language itself is what speaks, in the impersonal form of an anonymous babble. It is as if discourse were split into two non-overlapping figures, formed by the speaking subject and a 'double' – who does not have the reassuring name or transcendent face of the second person, but, as in Blanchot's *Très-Haut*, "he is a faceless, gazeless *he* who can only see through the language of another whom he submits to the order of his own night."[74]

However, this gutted stage of great contemporary literature, now bereft of authors and works, is precisely what allows a fundamental difficulty to emerge into view, a constitutive aporia that affects the entire theory of statements. Contemporary literature, radically outward-facing as it has been described, creates a displacement of the person into the non-linguistic sphere of the impersonal. The *he/she* – or the 'one' – is the estranged space in which the being of language discloses its irreducibility to the horizontal plane on which the dialogue between *I* and *thou* [*tu*], or between *we* and *you* [*voi*], is located. And yet this non-linguisticity remains locked inside a writing, itself inevitably linguistic in nature, that serves as its vehicle. Indeed, precisely in order to escape the referential logic of intersubjective communication, language is identified with writing: writing expresses nothing outside of writing itself. But if this is the case, if writing is always writing about writing, then, evidently, the outside of literature has the form of an inside; it never crosses over its own pre-established confines. When Foucault writes that "today's writing has freed itself from the theme of expression. Referring only to itself, but without being restricted to the confines of its interiority, writing is identified with its own unfolded exteriority,"[75] it would appear he had sensed the problem but was unable to resolve it exclusively within the enunciative field. As we saw earlier, this is parallel to the problem of visibility, in the sense that the being of language is never coextensive with that of light. But how do we pass from one to the other? How do we see what we talk about, or talk about what we see? How can the exteriority of a sphere escape even outside itself, so as to form relations with the sphere of the other? Or, to express it differently, what lies outside the outside? To answer this question, Foucault picks up on Nietzsche's concept of force. It is the axis of force – or rather of forces, since a force is such only if it is related to other forces, strengthening or weakening them – that constitutes the point of intersection and tension between the form of the statement and that of visibility: precisely because it is exterior not only to the double exteriority of seeing and speaking, but also to itself. Deleuze explains this subtle but crucial difference:

> We must distinguish between exteriority and the outside. Exteriority is still a form, as in *The Archaeology of Knowledge* – even two forms which are exterior to one another, since knowledge is made from the two environments of light and language, seeing and speaking. But the outside concerns force: if force is always in relation with other forces, forces necessarily refer to an irreducible outside which no longer even has any form and is made up of distances that cannot be broken down through which one force acts upon another or is acted upon by another.[76]

Thus in Foucault's work, the archive, that is, the history of forms, is doubled by the becoming of forces, expressed instead by the diagram. Except that the diagram meets up not only with the outside, but with the outside of the outside, looking out, as Herman Melville said, onto that "oceanic" line that passes under hurricanes, twisting around itself until it touches the extremity of the outer extremity, the *absolute* outside.

But what exactly is the absolute outside? What is more outside than the outside, or at a further extremity than the extremity? What force, in other words, has enough force to tip over into its opposite, even while resisting it? In *The Order of Things*, this vortex has the enigmatic name of the unthought: what precedes thought in a way that eludes any reflection, because it is what thought ensues from. In later texts, although he continues to elaborate on this first connotation that he never abandons, Foucault also begins – bit by bit, and then more and more – to shift it toward the category of life. Deleuze once again puts us on the right track when he observes that an outside further away than any external world and than any form of exteriority can only be an inside that lies deeper than any internal world: "The outside is not a fixed limit but a moving matter animated by peristaltic movements, folds and foldings that together make up an inside: they are not something other than the outside, but precisely the inside *of* the outside."[77] The reason why this outside is so elusive is that somehow, and without diminishing its degree of extraneity in any way, it lies within us: we ourselves are looked at from a point of view that does not coincide, and indeed collides, with the transcendental point of view of our person, which flows out onto the radically immanent plane of the impersonal. What is it that we are – beyond or before our person – without ever being able to become masters of it? What is it that traverses us and troubles us, to the point of turning over into its opposite, if not life itself? Indeed, in *The Order of Things*, life (together with language and labor) is the wavering line along which the outside folds over on itself, like the lining of a fabric or the invagination of embryological tissue: "life, on the confines of being, is what is exterior to it and also at the same time, what manifests itself within it."[78] It lies both in the depths of my being, to the point of being nothing other than me, and outside it, like a beam of light that illuminates me while pushing me at the same time toward the darkness: "Can I say that I am this life I sense deep within me, but which envelops

me both in the irresistible time that grows side by side with it and
poses me for a moment on its crest, and in the imminent time that
prescribes my death?"[79]

Already in this text, life is the moving edge along which human
beings battle against something that both constitutes them and
threatens them – what Bichat recognized as the front line of resistance against the dull roar of death. Fundamentally, it recalls both
Melville's oceanic line – which, like a boat adrift, "goes into hor-
rible contortions when that moment comes, and always runs the
risk of sweeping someone away with it" – and Michaux's line " 'of
a thousand aberrations' with its growing molecular speed, which
is the 'whiplash of a furious charioteer.' "[80] But it is especially in
the cycle opened up by *The Will to Knowledge* and in the seminars
Foucault gave on biopolitics during the same period that life, in
its simple biological structure, became the ultimate and primary
ground of a battle spurring human beings toward a limit point, a
battle in which the most extreme risk is united with the most
unprecedented of opportunities. The semantic confine between
these two possibilities, which is at play here, is once again traced
out by the ambivalent profile of the person. As we saw in the
earlier chapters of this book, the individual, understood as the site
of imputation of a legal personality, is the privileged subject of
biopolitical deconstruction. Its most significant meaning or effect
lies in the replacement, or at least marginalization, of the person
in favor of an individual or collective substance rooted in the
ground of biological life. Power, writes Foucault, "would no
longer be dealing simply with legal subjects over whom the ultimate dominion was death, but with living beings, and the mastery
it would be able to exercise over them would have to be applied
at the level of life itself."[81] This does not mean, he continues, that
the law and legal institutions would disappear; but their functions
would be increasingly directed toward normalization, through a
series of medical and administrative apparatuses aimed at regulat-
ing the population as a whole: "a normalizing society is the historical outcome of a technology of power centered on life. We
have entered a phase of juridical regression in comparison with
the pre-seventeenth societies we are familiar with."[82] The constitu-
tions and codes that followed each other at an increasing pace
beginning in the early 1800s were the balancing mechanisms that

made possible a normalizing type of power. We have followed the thanatopolitical drift that this process gave rise to during the period of Nazism. The destruction of the legal person, in those circumstances, became the pedestal of an immense sacrificial pyramid, on whose slopes millions of deaths were amassed. However, as we have seen from a longer-term perspective, the reason for this deadly outcome owes less to the deconstruction of the category of person initiated in the previous century than it does to the persistence of its exclusionary dispositif, which endured even in the efforts to abolish it.

This last step on the reasoning path – along with the unconcealment of the reifying logic of the person – lies outside Foucault's intellectual journey, which was limited to the conceptual formulation of the biopolitical paradigm. This does not detract from the fact that, through this paradigm, he identified – in life, and more specifically in its opposition to the compass of the law – a disruptive element overlapping, sometimes indistinguishably, the prescriptive dynamics of biopower. Without forcing Foucault's work in the direction of an affirmative biopolitics, but without losing the extraordinary power of its conceptual impact either, this ambivalence can be traced back to the inseparability it has always affirmed between the exercise of power and resistance – not only in the sense that they respond to each other, but also, and especially, in what ensues from this inseparability: power is what generates the resistance of that onto which it discharges itself. This explains why life, distinct from the subjectivity of the person as that which both underlies and overturns it into its material exteriority, constitutes the object of biopower, but also the locus that most opposes it.

Moreover, against this power that was still new in the nineteenth century, the forces that resisted relied for support on the very thing it invested, that is, on life and man as a living being. Since the last century the great struggles that have challenged the general system of power were not guided by the belief in a return to former rights [...]; what was demanded and what served as an objective was life, understood as the basic needs, man's concrete essence, the realization of his potential, a plenitude of the possible.[83]

As Foucault maintained in *The Order of Things*, only in recent times (and certainly not forever) has humanity constituted the mode of personhood – allied with other forces of finitude, like language and labor – through which life has expressed itself in its greatest plenitude. This does not mean that a time should come, or could be imagined, in which life labors or speaks against (or even in the absence of) humankind. But it can certainly be concluded that the person is not to be conceived of as the only form within which life is destined to flow. We may equally infer that life is inclined to break down its formal embankments in favor of collective needs and desires, which subjective rights are incapable of representing. That is why "life as a political object was in a sense taken at face value and turned back against the system it was bent on controlling. It was life more than the law that became the issue of political struggles, even if the latter were formulated through affirmations concerning rights."[84] An intrinsic relationship between humanity and rights, one that is freed from the subjective slant of the legal person and brought back to the singular, impersonal being of community, is only conceivable starting from life. How this may come to be, what steps this 'law in common' may entail, Foucault does not say. In fact, one might even imagine that the creative crisis he went through at the end of the 1970s stemmed partially from his inability to respond to these questions; more specifically, from the impression he received of not being able to break through the 'line of the outside' toward an area not yet occupied by diagrams of power; from the fear, more than justified, that life – the life that he sought in the folds and in the no-longer-such of the person – was nothing but a break in the march of death, an empty place in the procession of 'One dies.'[85]

"I will be told: 'That's so like you, always with the same inability to cross the line, to pass to the other side, to listen and convey the language that comes from elsewhere or from below,'" he warns the reader in one of his most powerful essays, devoted to the "Lives of Infamous Men." The extreme direction his discourse was taking before it was interrupted clearly indicates that his subject was life. But the fact that the life we are talking about is of people who are literally nameless and faceless, without any of the attributes that make up the rational, social, and legal baggage of personhood, makes this text Foucault's deepest foray into the impenetrable and perilous terrain of the impersonal. The essay was the introduction to a planned anthology of short documents, dating between the second half of the seventeenth century and the first half of the eighteenth, taken from the archives of internment at the General Hospital and the Bastille: mostly *lettres de cachet*, petitions to the king, and prison or death sentences. Lives that were wretched, confined, and almost always iniquitous, then. Lowly, lost lives reduced to a handful of ashes – but also "flash existences" and "poem-lives" brought for a moment to the center-stage of the chronicle, out of the momentary and always traumatic clash with a power that awaited them at the pass, persecuted them, and then extinguished them. In this way alone, through this ring of captivity and suffering, of withering away or terror, were these lives that were initially fated to pass beneath any sort of discourse able to leave a trace, one that is sometimes faint and at times more deeply etched, but in all instances disturbing. What counts is that these lives, never having played a prominent subjective role, slipping through the nets of history, so to speak, and lost in the anonymity of existence, never speak in the first person, never pronounce the pronoun *I*, and never address themselves to a *you*. They are nothing but facts or events in the third person, passed down to us purely as a result of unexpected circumstances, an accident of nature, or the whim of a king. Nothing is more distant, in them, than the light surrounding the heroes of politics and history dear to Hannah Arendt – the protagonists or antagonists who cross paths and clash with each other in the daylight-flooded world of the public sphere. Contrary to any 'fame,' they are literally infamous. They are people of the night: "Lives that are as though they hadn't been, that survive only from the clash with a power that wished only to annihilate them or at least to obliterate them, lives that come back to us only through the effect of multiple accidents."[86] Yet nothing captured the gaze of Foucault as much as these lives bereft of any brilliance or form; nothing made such an intense physical impression on him, or made him vibrate so violently as they did. Not just because of the striking lack of proportion that exists between the dullness of these insignificant existences and the theatrical solemnity of the power that struck them down. But because of the passion, the energy, and the excess that life – when viewed from the other side of the mirror, from the side external to the line of the outside – evokes when it is no longer trapped in the metaphysics of the person, when it remains extraneous to its exclusionary effect, and it dully but obstinately clings only to itself.


## 7  The Event

The most compelling encounter between contemporary philosophy and the power of the impersonal is certainly to be found in the work of Gilles Deleuze. All the figures we have isolated so far – Kojève's animal, Blanchot's neuter, and Foucault's outside – find their ideal congealing point in Deleuze's systematic destruction of the category of person in all its possible expressions. Unlike the previous thinkers, he does not approach his task by simply substituting one person for another, or by creating a triangulation that opens up the dialogue between two terms to the diagonal presence of a third. What he does instead is to rotate the entire philosophical horizon toward a theory of the pre-individual, impersonal event. This cannot be reduced to the personality of the subject of enunciation, or to the objectivity of a state of things introduced into a chain of causes and effects, or to the universal generality of an abstract concept. It does not involve designation, manifestation or signification, and it avoids falling into the alternatives between internal and external, particular and general, or individual and collective. It is essentially neutral with regard to all these oppositions – like a battle situated above the field where it is fought, indifferent to the fate of the winners and losers, perpetually suspended between what has happened and what may happen. Or like a wound carved into the body of someone who senses it as something other than their self, and yet inseparable from their flesh. This does not mean, for Deleuze, that the subject completely disappears, or that it becomes an inert container or a passive spectator of the event that is discharged on it. On the contrary, the formula he repeats on several occasions invites each one of us to be worthy of what happens to us. It also points to a more complex conception, according to which the individual on the one hand is identified with the impersonal event, but on the other is able to hold his or her own and turn it against itself in a "counter-actualization," as he expresses it. Playing with the temporal bifurcation – between a past never completed and a future yet to come – that every event bears within itself, the individual can unleash, in what occurs, the eventful power [*potenza evenemenziale*] enclosed inside it. This involves adhering so closely to the event, identifying so entirely with it, that we can drag it beyond its natural outcome and twist it into a different logic. His example of the actor is to be understood in this light: when actors interpret their role, they anticipate something yet to occur, or they reproduce an event that has already occurred, thus representing what, in that moment, is never present. Since the way the events are reproduced always extends out of their actual reality, one becomes "the actor of one's own events."[87] The actor actualizes events by counter-actualizing them, by entering into opposition with their original meaning or duplicating it, in an excess that transforms the meaning into its opposite. This is what occurs with death, the event par excellence, in which each of us is lost while at the same time causing death itself to be lost the instant it occurs. Or with life, which traverses and defines us as that which is most impersonal, given that every aspect of it eludes our control, but also as that which is most unique, since nobody will ever be able to replicate it in its absolute unicity.

Precisely because it is impersonal, the event coincides, in short, with an outflowing of singularities that have neither the apperceptive form of the *I* nor the transcendental form of consciousness. This is what Deleuze defines as the plane of immanence, meaning a sphere of life that is entirely coextensive with itself – in which the cause is one with its effect, so to speak, and the actor with what is acted upon. Hence the fact that the entire philosophical tradition has found the event inconceivable and has always been inclined to translate it (and thus to betray it) into a subjective or objective form, as a defense against the undifferentiated. Whether this form is given the character of a Being fully determined by its concept, or that of a person (divine or human) as the bearer of meaning, it still remains locked in an alternative between the bottomlessness of absolute indifference and the forced closure of singularity in the predefined perimeter of the individual. This is a bipolarity without issue, fixed not only by the philosophical tradition, but also – in different ways – by theology, cosmology, and psychology. The latter, in its Freudian and then Lacanian versions of psychoanalysis, is what comes under a no-holds-barred attack by Deleuze in his *Anti-Oedipus*. What ends up being deconstructed by this onslaught is the Oedipal triangulation – mother, father and son – which cages the production of desire, neutralizing it, inside figural forms of persons with a mythological character. In this case, too, personification, which brings the flows and pulsions of the real onto the plane of the symbolic and the imaginary, is justified by the need to erect embankments so as to contain the otherwise destructive power of chaos. But the threat of the undifferentiated is only the secondary product, or the reversed projection, of the differentiation of persons. Similarly, persons do not set up prohibitions, but rather the prohibitions – the law that prevents desire from being discharged – require figures in the form of persons capable of representing them on the Oedipal stage. In this manner a family regime that conjugates persons is substituted for the free circulation of 'partial objects,' foreclosing it. These partial objects are removed from the multiplicity of impersonal flows and locked up in the transcendental cage of a general signifier that both distributes the meanings and forces them into a hierarchy. In this way the paranoid–segregative pole of delirium prevails over the schizo-nomadic pole through the exclusionary circuit of the law, lack, and the signifier. In addition, Deleuze identifies in the Oedipal law the general structure of exclusion, but – what is even more important for our inquiry – he traces it back to the juridical dispositif of the person as formulated in Roman law. Precisely this, its presumed distance from the movement of bodies, produces the reifying effect of possession – depersonalization, that is – later inherited and perfected by the modern conception:

> The reason is that persons are derived from abstract quantities, instead of from flows. Instead of a connective appropriation, partial objects become the possessions of a person and, when required, the property of another person. Just as he draws upon centuries of scholastic reflection in defining God as the principle of the disjunctive syllogism, Kant draws upon centuries of Roman juridical reflection when he defines marriage as the tie that makes a person the owner of the sexual organs of another person.[88]

The only avenue for escaping the dialectic between personalization and depersonalization, which we are by now familiar with, passes through the deconstruction of the category of person, following a logic that privileges multiplicity and contamination over identity and discrimination. The Deleuzian concept of 'body without organs' must be understood in this light – one that is critical of the idea of person as owner of one's own organs, and at the same time as an organic body separate from the person that inhabits it. In the *Anti-Oedipus*, the area that comes primarily under this attack is the unconscious: it is removed from the personal protection of the 'holy family' and returned to the impersonal flow of desiring-machines. But in subsequent texts, and in particular in his *Essays Critical and Clinical*, the deconstruction extends on a broader horizon, which includes the sphere of language and literature. In contrast to the psychoanalytical tendency of defining the indeterminate through the use of the personal or the possessive, literature runs in the opposite direction, going back to the indeterminate source of that which is caged in the block of the definition. This is also how the language of children operates: they prefer to express themselves using nouns preceded by the indefinite article: *a* father, *a* body or *a* horse, rather than my father, my body or my horse. This does not lead to any loss in expressive quality, since the indefinite does not lack definition – just that its particular determination is not the static one of being, but the fluid one of becoming or, in fact, of the impersonal. From this point of view the relationship, already remarked on by Blanchot, that literature has with the third person is confirmed:

> But literature takes the opposite path, and exists only when it discovers beneath apparent persons the power of an impersonal – which is not a generality but a singularity at the highest point: a man, a woman, a beast, a stomach, a child … It is not the first two persons that function as the condition for literary enunciation; literature begins only when a third person is born in us that strips us of the power to say 'I' (Blanchot's 'neuter').[89]

Here Deleuze seems to open a polemical front against the theory of Benveniste – with which we, too, began – on the enunciative incapacity of the third person, and hence on its impossibility of being defined as such. In reality, by placing literature outside of, and against, the laws of linguistics, by pushing it onto the plane of the asyntactic, and even of the agrammatical, Deleuze only ends up confirming the theory, and even taking it to its extreme consequences: the countering force of literary writing lies in its reversal of a rule – the one established by Benveniste – that applies to all other types of interlocution. Literature speaks in the third person because its utterances enounce nothing or, more precisely, what it utters is nothingness, since it is addressed to no one, except perhaps to those who place themselves on the outer confines of language. This movement of exteriorization, or estrangement, is the salient character of true literature: at least beginning with Proust, a writer is someone who drags a language out of its ruts, making it literally 'delirious' by opening it up and turning it inside out like a glove. This can be done either by introducing a foreign language inside the writer's mother tongue, or the other way round, by transferring the mother tongue into the vocabulary of a foreign language. While Melville insinuates the foreign, even inhuman language of the whale into English, Wolfson converts phrases of his own language into different linguistic syntagms, while Raymond Roussel excavates homophonic series out of his native French that are equivalent to the presence of another language. Martin Heidegger and Alfred Jarry – whom Deleuze juxtaposes in a dizzying comparison – use yet another alienating technique, which is that of playing with a dead language in a living one, with the effect of making them both vacillate. The language is made to sway, twitch, and crack until it explodes into a new linguistic entity. It even produces something that is not precisely a language, something falling short of, or beyond, a language, because the visions and sounds it produces do not really belong to the vocal form: they are rather strips of reality that the writer sees and hears through the openings in language, not as interruptions to the process, but as "an eternity that can only be revealed in a becoming or a landscape that only appears in movement. They are not outside language, but the outside of language. The writer as seer and hearer, the aim of literature: it is the passage of life within language that constitutes Ideas."[90]

Life itself (*a* life, as Deleuze entitled the last essay he left us)[91] is the term that would seem to sum up the entire theory of the impersonal, extending it into a form that is still indeterminate and, for this very reason, bursting with unexpressed potential. Life is the tangent, the line of force, along which immanence folds back on itself, eliding any form of transcendence or any ulteriority beyond being a living substance as such. It refers neither to a rational subject nor to a bare material substrate. But above all, if understood in its impersonal, singular dimension,[92] life is what does not allow – what contradicts at its roots – the hierarchical division between these two entities within the separating dispositif of the person. This is what sets it at such a radical distance – or shifts it to such a different plane, if you will – with respect to the entire conceptual apparatus of modern political philosophy. We have seen how modern philosophy makes the possibility of order dependent on an interaction between subjects who are characterized as being split between a site of legal imputation and a corporeal area subject to its control. Whether this control passes through a sovereign mediation of an external nature or is entrusted to the will of the individual owner, the body remains exposed to a mechanism of appropriation, disassemblage, and manipulation that ends up assimilating the body to a thing owned by others or by itself. Even the semantics of the Catholic discourse on the inaccessibility of life – its absolute value deriving from the act of a Creator who maintains possession over it – remains within the same paradigm. The body is always at the disposal of a person, whether divine or human, who is not coextensive with it and whose transcendence in relation to the body is actually the basis of its definition. The very fact that whoever comes into the world is declared to be a person – sooner or later, but always on the basis of certain scientific, ethical, or religious protocols – implies its difference of principle from the vital substratum into which it is implanted.

In contrast with this dualistic model, Deleuze works along a path that is both deconstructive and affirmative, and reaches its apex in *A Thousand Plateaus*. This path is divided into three strategic levels, which correspond to the three-pronged attack he conducts against the concept of person. The first, a necessary premise for the other two, involves replacing the category of possibility with that of virtuality, a process initiated by Bergson. While this first move reappears, albeit in different ways, in all philosophies whose premises are cast in a Schellingian mold, the second is the only one not to betray its immanence, resolving the origin as part of the process of ontological constitution. Against the founding distinction between possible and real – which, for example, sees in the embryo a potential person but not an actual one, thus leaving it in a zone of theoretical indistinguishability and making it accessible to biopolitics – Deleuze assigns the same status to the virtual as he does to reality, relating it more to the actual. Life, as such and in all its manifestations, is always real, even though it individuates itself into forms that, at each occurrence, actualize what is still virtual at an earlier stage. This does not mean that all reality is actual, or that the actual is the only mode of the real – this would mean blocking the process of individuation into sclerotic, immobile forms. Indeed, like in Gilbert Simondon's ontogenetic theory (according to which every new individuation always preserves a pre-individual element that pushes the individual outside its confines), in Deleuze's theory, too, there always remains a portion of the virtual that precedes or exceeds the full actualization. There is no key moment at which something ceases to be possible in order to become real, because at all times the real retains a zone of virtuality. A being is constituted precisely by this oscillation between actual and virtual – between order and chaos, between identity and transformation, between form and force – which, by keeping that being in perpetual tension with itself, translates it into becoming.

The second line of attack against the person passes through the concept of individuation, which is shifted from the horizon of the subject to that of life. The individuation of life, of a life, is not the same as the individuation of a personal subject. The category of 'haecceity' intervenes between the two. It, too, designates something – individuating it – that is very particular, but not necessarily a person, a thing, or a substance. A season or a time of day, for example, are haecceities that are just as determinate as individuals as such; but they are not coextensive with them – just like a shower of rain, a gust of wind, or a ray of moonlight. What these connote, besides their movement due to the combination of their molecules, is a capacity to be composed with other forces, due to which they undergo an effect (or an affect), thereby being transformed and transforming the others into more complex individualities, themselves subject to the possibility of further metamorphoses. A degree of temperature can be combined with a certain intensity of whiteness, just as this may combine with a surface to the point of being identified with it. What changes with respect to the plane of the subjects, besides a certain spatiality that is irreducible to predefined boundaries, is a temporality that does not have the stable form of presence, but rather the form of the event, extending between past and future. Haecceity never has an origin or an end – it is not a point: it is a line of slippage and assemblage [*concatenamento*]. It is made up not of people and things, but of speeds, affects, and transitions; just as its semiotics is composed of proper nouns, verbs in the infinitive, and indefinite pronouns. Haecceity is composed of third persons, traversed and liberated by the power of the impersonal:

> The HE does not represent a subject but rather makes a diagram of an assemblage. It does not overcode statements, it does not transcend them as do the first two persons; on the contrary, it prevents them from falling under the tyranny of subjective or signifying constellations, under the regime of empty redundancies.[93]

Not you and I, then – not proprietary subjects and dominated bodies – but 'a Hans to become horse,' 'a mute named wolf,' 'wasp to meet orchid.'

Here we come to the final station on the path, the last point of the controversial constellation created by Deleuze with regard to the person as an exclusive and exclusionary form of being: the experience of "becoming-animal," in which the movement of concepts outlined thus far achieves its greatest density. Deleuze's becoming-animal takes on its full constitutive and countering force when we recall that the animalization of man was the most devastating outcome of the dispositif of the person, but also of the thanatopolitical powers that imagined they were opposing it while actually enhancing its coercive power. In a theological, philosophical, and political tradition that has always defined the human through opposition to the animal – to that part of the human, or that area of humanity, that was bestialized as a prophylactic measure – the vindication of animality as our most intimate nature breaks with a fundamental interdiction that has always ruled over us. Becoming-animal, for Deleuze, does not signify sinking into the darkest pit of the human being; nor is it a metaphor or a literary phantasm. On the contrary, it is our most tangible reality, so long as what we mean by real is the process of mutation that our nature has always undergone. What we are talking about is not humankind's *alter*, or the *alter* in humankind, but rather humankind brought back to its natural alteration. The animal – in the human, of the human – means above all multiplicity, plurality, assemblage with what surrounds us and with what always dwells inside us: "We do not become an animal without a fascination for the pack, for multiplicity. A fascination for the outside? Or is the multiplicity that fascinates us already related to a multiplicity dwelling within us?"[94] But this also means plurivocity, metamorphosis, contamination – and preventive critique of any claim to hereditary, ethnic, or racial purity. In opposition to purity, against its supposed immune effects, the becoming-animal becomes "propagation by epidemic, by contagion, [which] has nothing to do with filiation by heredity."[95] The difference is that, unlike blood affiliations and racial memberships, it brings into relationship completely heterogeneous terms – like a human being, an animal, and a microorganism; but even a tree, a season, and an atmosphere: because what matters in the becoming-animal, even before its relationship with the animal, is especially the becoming of a life that only individuates itself by breaking the chains and prohibitions, the barriers and boundaries, that the human has etched within it. Whence the return of the association between impersonal and singular that can only be grasped through a radical rethinking of the category of person. Not, as we have said repeatedly, by simply negating it but, if anything, by freeing the exclusionary and reifying form inside of which our tradition has sealed off its meaning. The becoming-animal of the human points to the unraveling of this metaphysical node, to a way of being human that is not coextensive with the person or the thing, or with the perpetual transfer between one and the other that we appear to have been fated to until now. It is the *living person* – not separate from or implanted into life, but coextensive with it as an inseparable *synolon* of form and force, external and internal, *bios* and *zoe*. The third person, this figure that has yet to be fathomed, points to this *unicum*, to this being that is both singular and plural – to the non-person inscribed in the person, to the person open to what has never been before.

# Notes

## Notes to Introduction

1   M. Zambrano, *Persona y democracia. La historia sacrificial*, Departamento de Instrucción Pública: San Juan de Puerto Rico, 1958; Italian version *Persona e democrazia. La storia sacrificale*, Mondadori: Milan 2000, p. 148. [Translator's Note: All quotations from Italian and French texts not available in English have been translated by me. Where English translations exist, I have used those editions and cited them in the bibliography, sometimes after the original reference, or, in cases where standard editions exist for well-known authors, I have provided only the authorized English edition. For quotations from texts originally in languages other than Italian or French where no English translation exists, I have translated from the Italian into English and provided the reference from the original-language text.]

2   P. Ricoeur, "Meurt le personnalisme, revient la personne …," in *Esprit*, 1, 1983, pp. 113–19; Italian version *La persona*, Morcelliani: Brescia 1997, pp. 21–36.

3   See especially R. de Monticelli, *La conoscenza personale. Introduzione alla fenomenologia*, Cortina: Milan 1998; R. de Monticelli (ed.), *Testi fenomenologici 1911–1933*, Cortina: Milan 2000.

4   A useful overview of the various notions of person as framed in the English-speaking world is provided by M. di Francesco, *L'io e i suoi sé. Identità personale e scienza della mente*, Cortina: Milan 1998. For a different approach to the question, see the highly informative book by R. Bodei, *Destini personali. L'età della colonizzazione delle coscienze*, Feltrinelli: Milan 2002.

5 I'm thinking especially about the insightful essay by E. Severino, *Sull'embrione*, Rizzoli: Milan 2005 – which fails, however, to penetrate the "black box" of personhood.

6 S. Benhabib, *The Rights of Others: Aliens, Residents and Citizens*, Cambridge University Press: Cambridge and New York 2004. See, in a similar line of thought, R. Finelli, F. Fistetti, F. R. Luciani, and P. Di Vittorio (eds.), *Globalizzazione e diritti umani*, Manifestolibri: Rome 2004. N. Irti offers a different and original perspective, informed by the new dynamics of biopolitics, in "La giuridificazione del bios," *Communitas*, 6, 2005, pp. 35–40.

7 See M. Nussbaum, *Giustizia sociale e dignità umana. Da individui a persone*, Il Mulino: Bologna 2002; Nussbaum, *Women and Human Development: The Capabilities Approach*, Cambridge University Press: Cambridge and New York 2000.

8 L. Ferrajoli, *Diritti fondamentali*, Laterza: Rome, Bari 2001, p. 23.

9 S. Rodotà, *La vita e le regole. Tra diritto e non diritto*, Feltrinelli: Milan 2006, p. 25.

10 Ibid., p. 32.

11 See E. Levinas, *Quelques réflexions sur la philosophie de l'hitlérisme* [1934], edited by M. Abensour, Paris 1997. Italian edition *Alcune riflessioni sulla filosofia dell'hitlerismo*, Quodlibet: Macerata 1997.

12 The study by Y. Thomas, "Le Sujet de droit, la personne et la nature," *Le Débat*, 100 (May–August 1998), pp. 85–107, is crucial to an understanding of Roman law, as is Thomas's "Le Sujet concret et sa personne. Essai d'histoire juridique rétrospective," in O. Cayla and Y. Thomas, *Du droit de ne pas naître*, Gallimard: Paris 2002, pp. 91–170.

13 On the contemporary strategies of depersonalization, see also A. dal Lago, *Non persone. L'esclusione dei migranti in una società globale*, Feltrinelli: Milan 1999.

14 In this regard, see issue 0 (2006) of the journal *Fata Morgana* – an issue dedicated to the relationship between cinema and biological life – and especially the paper by P. Montani, *Estetica, tecnica e biopolitica*, pp. 27–55.

## Notes to Chapter 1

1 X. Bichat, *Recherches physiologiques sur la vie et sur la mort* [1800], Geneva, Paris, Brussels 1962, p. 43; quoted from the English edition *Physiological Researches upon Life and Death*, trans. Tobias Watkins, Smith & Maxwell: Philadelphia 1809, p. 1.

2 Ibid., pp. 43–4.

3   G. Canguilhem, *Claude Bernard et Bichat*, in *Études d'histoire et de philosophie des sciences concernant les vivants et la vie*, Paris 1994, p. 158.

4   X. Bichat, *Anatomie générale appliquée à la physiologie et à la médecine*, Paris 1801, vol. 1, p. 99; quoted from the English translation, *General Anatomy, Applied to Physiology and Medicine*, vol. 1, trans. George Hayward, Richardson and Lord: Boston 1822, p. 60.

5   See Michel Foucault, *Naissance de la clinique. Une archéologie du regard médical*, Paris 1963; English version *The Birth of the Clinic: An Archaeology of Medical Perception* [1973], trans. A. M. Sheridan, Vintage Books: New York 1994, p. 144.

6   The importance of the survival of organic life versus animal life in Bichat was highlighted by Giorgio Agamben in *Quel che resta di Auschwitz*, Turin 1998, pp. 141–4; English version *Remnants of Auschwitz*, Zone Books: Brooklyn 1999.

7   Translator's note: in Italian as in English, the participle 'decided' (*deciso*) derives from the Latin *decidere* ('to terminate'/'to determine'), which is in turn a compound of *caedere* ('to cut') with the deverbative prefix *de*. Hence this equivalence.

8   Arthur Schopenhauer, *Die Welt als Wille und Vorstellung*, in *Werke*, Zürich 1988; quoted from the English version *The World as Will and Representation*, trans. E. F. J. Payne, vol. 2, Dover Publications: New York 1966, pp. 264–5. For more on Schopenhauer's relation to Bichat, see also S. Barbera, *Il mondo come volontà e rappresentazione*, Rome 1998, pp. 183ff.

9   Schopenhauer, *The World as Will and Representation*, p. 261.

10  Arthur Schopenhauer, *The World as Will and Idea*, vol. 1, trans. Haldane and Kemp, Trubner & Co.: Ludgate Hill, London 1883, p. 192.

11  For an acute biopolitical or 'bioeconomic' reading of Schopenhauer, see Laura Bazzicalupo, *Il governo delle vite. Biopolitica ed economia*, Rome, Bari 2006, pp. 77–8.

12  Schopenhauer, *The World as Will and Idea*, vol. 1, p. 191.

13  Ibid., p. 437.

14  Ibid., p. 452.

15  Auguste Comte, *Système de politique positive ou Traité de sociologie instituant la religion de l'humanité*, Paris 1969 (anastatic facsimile of the 1851–4 edn.), vol. 1, pp. 618–19.

16  Ibid., p. 600.

17  Ibid., pp. 484, 473.

18  Auguste Comte, *Cours de philosophie positive*, Paris 1968 (anastatic facsimile of the 1893 edn.), vol. 3, pp. 224–6.

19  Auguste Comte, *System of Positive Polity*, vol. 1, Longmans, Green, and Co.: London 1875, pp. 289–90.

20  For this interpretation of Comte, see the important monograph by B. Karsenti, *Politique de l'esprit. Comte et la naissance de la science sociale*, Paris 2006.

21  Comte, *System of Positive Polity*, vol. 1, p. 518.

22  *The Positive Philosophy of Auguste Comte*, trans. Harriet Martineau, vol. 2, John Chapman: London 1853, p. 102.

23  Ibid., p. 103.

24  Victor Courtet de l'Isle, *La Science politique fondée sur la science de l'homme ou Étude des races humaines*, Paris 1937, p. ix.

25  Ibid., p. 139.

26  Ibid., p. viii.

27  See C.-B. Dunoyer, *L'Industrie et la morale considérées dans leurs rapports avec la liberté*, Paris 1825.

28  See especially Patrick Tort, *La Pensée et l'évolution hiérarchique*, Paris 1983.

29  See Charles Lyell, *The Geological Evidences of the Antiquity of Man with Remarks on Theories of the Origin of Species by Variation*, London 1963, especially chapter 23 on the comparison of the origin and development of languages and species.

30  A. Schleicher, *Sprachvergleichende Untersuchungen*, vol. 1: *Zur vergleichenden Sprachengeschichte*, Bonn 1848.

31  A. Schleicher, *Die Sprachen Europas in systematischer Übersicht*, Bonn 1850.

32  Schleicher, *Sprachvergleichende Untersuchungen*, vol. 1, p.1.

33  A. Schleicher, *Die deutsche Sprache*, Stuttgart 1860.

34  A. Schleicher, *Die darwinsche Theorie und die Sprachwissenschaft. Offenes Sendschreiben an Herrn Dr. Ernst Häckel*, Weimar 1863; English version *Darwinism Tested by the Science of Language*, trans. Alex V. W. Bikkers, John Camden Hotten: Piccadilly 1869.

35  A. Schleicher, *Über die Bedeutung der Sprache für die Naturgeschichte des Menschen*, Weimar 1965.

36  Ibid. I quote from the modern edition of a French translation of Schleicher's work cited in n. 35 above: *De l'Importance du langage pour l'histoire naturelle de l'homme*, in P. Tort, *Évolutionnisme et linguistique*, Paris 1980, pp. 83–5.

37  Schleicher, *Die Sprachen Europas in systematischer Übersicht*, p. 14.

38  On this intertwining between linguistics and anthropology, see the extensive reconstruction by A. Morpurgo Davies, *La linguistica dell'Ottocento*, Bologna 1996, pp. 217ff.

39  P. Broca, *La Linguistique et l'anthropologie* [1862], in *Mémoires d'anthropologie*, Paris 1871, vol. 1, pp. 232–76.

40  A. Pictet, *Les Origines indo-européennes ou les Aryas primitifs. Essai de paléontologie linguistique*, Paris 1859–63, vol. 1, p. 14.

41  M. Müller, *Lectures in the Science of Language Delivered at the Royal Institution of Great Britain in April, May, & June 1861*, London 1961, pp. 74–5.

42  H.-J. Chavée, *Les Langues et les races*, Paris 1962, pp. 7–8.

43  Ibid., p. 10.

44  Ibid., p. 13.

45  See A. Hovelacque, *La Linguistique. Histoire naturelle du langage*, Paris 1877, p. 403.

46  On the two 'chosen' languages, see M. Olender, *Les Langues du paradis: Aryens et Sémites, un couple providentiel*, Paris 1989.

47  E. Renan, *Histoire générale et système comparé des langues sémitiques*, Paris 1855. I quote from the 3rd edn., 1863, pp. 495–6. For a balanced assessment of Renan's role, see C. Vallini, *Renan tra filologia semitica e linguistica indoeuropea*, in G. Massariello Merzagora (ed.), *Storia del pensiero linguistico: linearità, fratture e circolarità*, Rome 2001, pp. 69–111.

48  From A. de Tocqueville's letter to A. de Gobineau, dated November 1, 1853, in A. de Tocqueville and A. de Gobineau, *Del razzismo. Carteggio 1843–1859*, ed. by L. Michelini Tocci, Rome, 1995, p. 167; quoted from the English edition *Selected Letters on Politics and Society*, ed. by Roger Boesche, University of California Press: Berkeley, Los Angeles, London 1985, p. 300.

49  A. de Gobineau, *Essai sur l'inégalité des races humaines*, in *Oeuvres*, Paris, 1983, vol. 1, pp. 141–2; English version *The Inequality of Human Races*, trans. Adrian Collins, G. P. Putnam's Sons: London 1915, p. 23.

50  Ibid., p. 24.

51  Ibid., p. 1152.

52  A. de Gobineau, *Mémoire sur diverses manifestations de la vie individuelle*, ed. by A. B. Duff, Paris 1935. The text was published in German under the title "Untersuchung über verschiedene Äusserungen des sporadischen Lebens," in *Zeitschrift für Philosophie und philosophische Kritik* 52, 1868, pp. 17–35, 181–204, and 53, 1868, pp. 1–41. The editor's reference to Schleicher is on p. 9. Regarding the *Mémoire*, see Tort, *La Pensée et l'évolution hiérarchique*, pp. 199ff.

53  Gobineau, *Mémoire sur diverses manifestations*, p. 114.

54  Ibid., p. 194.

55  Ibid., p. 112.

56  Ibid., p. 210.

57  On Haeckel's intellectual environment, see M. di Gregorio, *Entre Méphistophélès et Luther: Ernst Haeckel et la réforme de l'univers*, in P. Tort (ed.), *Darwinisme et société*, Paris 1992, pp. 237–83.

58  E. Haeckel, *Die Welträthsel. Gemeinverständliche Studien über monistische Philosophie*, Bonn 1899; English version *The Riddle of the Universe at the Close of the Nineteenth Century*, trans. Joseph McCabe, Harper & Brothers: New York 1900, pp. 7–8.

59  Ibid., p. 131.

60  E. Haeckel, *Natürliche Schöpfungsgeschichte*, Berlin 1868; English version *The History of Creation*, trans. E. Ray Lankester, D. Appleton and Company: New York 1876, vol. 2, pp. 492–3.

61  Ibid., p. 433.

62  E. Haeckel, *Freie Wissenschaft und freie Lehre*, Stuttgart 1878; English version *Freedom in Science and Teaching*, trans. T. H. Huxley, D. Appleton and Company: New York 1879.

63  Jena 1895.

64  Eisenach–Leipzig 1903.

65  See especially W. Schallmayer, *Vererbung und Auslese im Lebenslauf der Völker. Eine staatswissenschaftliche Studie auf Grund der neueren Biologie*, Jena 1903.

66  G. Vacher de Lapouge, *Race et milieu social. Essais d'Anthroposociologie*, Paris 1909, pp. xxii–xxiii.

67  G. Vacher de Lapouge, "Introduction," in E. Haeckel, *Le Monisme: lien entre la religion et la science*, Paris 1902, p. 2; German version *Der Monismus als Band zwischen Religion und Wissenschaft*, Bonn 1893.

68  G. Vacher de Lapouge, *L'Aryen: son rôle social*, Paris 1899, p. 512.

69  On this topic, see S. Strong, "Biopolitica delle anime," *Filosofia politica* 3, 2003, pp. 397–418.

70  C. Richet, *La Sélection humaine*, in *Eugénique et sélection*, Alcan: Paris 1922, p. 164.

71  A. Carrel, *L'Homme, cet inconnu*, Paris 1935, pp. 371–2; English version *Man, the Unknown*, Harper & Brothers: New York, 1939, p. 319.

72  A. Hoche, *Ärztliche Bemerkungen*, in K. Binding and A. Hoche, *Die Freigabe der Vernichtung lebensunwerten Lebens: Ihr Mass und ihre Form*, Leipzig 1920, pp. 61–2.

73  H. F. K. Günther, *Humanitas*, Munich 1937, p. 18.

74  For this interpretation of Nazism, see R. Esposito, *Bios. Biopolitica e filosofia*, Einaudi: Turin 2004, pp. 155 ff; English version *Bios: Biopolitics and Philosophy*, trans. Timothy Campbell, University of Minnesota Press: Minneapolis 2008.

75  V. Klemperer, *LTI. Notizbuch eines Philologen* [1947], Leipzig 1975. For more on this topic, see E. Cohen Dabah, *Il potere silenzioso del nazismo: la lingua del Terzo Reich*, in C.-C. Härle (ed.), *Shoah. Percorsi della memoria*, Naples 2006, pp. 65–79.

76  P. Levi, *The Drowned and the Saved*, trans. Raymond Rosenthal, Vintage International: New York 1989, p. 91.

77  On this topic, see the detailed analysis by D. Chiapponi, *La lingua nei lager nazisti*, Rome 2004, pp. 59ff.

78  The reference is to W. Oschlies, "'Lagerszpracha.' Zu Theorie und Empirie einer KZ-spezifischen Soziolinguistik," *Zeitgeschichte*, 13 (1), 1985, pp. 1–27.

79  P. Levi, *The Drowned and the Saved*, p. 99.

## Notes to Chapter 2

1  For an account of these events, see R. Overy, *Interrogations: The Nazi Elite in Allied Hands, 1945*, Penguin Books: New York 2001, pp. 3–24.

2  See Y. Ternon, *L'État criminel*, Paris 1995; Italian version *Lo stato criminale*, Milan 1997, pp. 24–34.

3  Among the many works on human rights, Slavoj Žižek's "Against Human Rights," *New Left Review*, 34, 2005, pp. 115–31, stands out for its clarity.

4  H. Arendt, *The Origins of Totalitarianism* [1951], Harcourt: New York 1966, pp. 299–300.

5  Ibid., p. 297.

6  Ibid., p. 286.

7  Jacques Maritain, *The Rights of Man and Natural Law*, trans. Doris C. Anson, Gordian Press: New York 1971, p. 65.

8  Ibid., p. 65.

9  As Marcel Mauss had already shown in "Une catégorie de l'esprit humain: la notion de personne, celle de 'moi,'" in *Journal of the Royal Anthropological Institute*, 68, 1938, pp. 263–83.

10  S. Schlossmann, *Persona und prosōpon im Recht und im christlichen Dogma*, Kiel 1906.

11  A. Prosperi, *Dare l'anima. Storia di un infanticidio*, Turin 2005, especially pp. 285–99.

12  For more on this topic, see H. Rheinfelder, *Das Wort Persona. Geschichte seiner Bedeutung mit besonderer Berücksichtigung des französischen und italienischen Mittelalters*, Halle 1928, pp. 180ff.

13  See Pietro Bonfante, *Il 'ius vendendi' del 'paterfamilias' e la legge 2, Codice 4, 43, di Costantino* [1906], in *Scritti giuridici varii*, Turin

1926, vol. 1, pp. 64ff.; and, also by Bonfante, *Corso di diritto romano. Della famiglia*, Pavia 1908, pp. 5ff. and 66ff.

14 For a rigorous, innovative genealogy of the Roman legal tradition, see the book by Aldo Schiavone, *The Invention of Law in the West*, trans. Jeremy Carden and Antony Shugaar, Harvard University Press: Cambridge, MA 2011. On the problematic nature of the concept of 'individual rights' in Roman law, see also E. Stolfi, "I 'diritti' a Roma," *Political Philosophy*, 3, 2005, pp. 383–98.

15 See Riccardo Orestano, *Il 'problema delle persone giuridiche' in diritto romano*, Turin 1968, pp. 12ff.

16 Another author who has worked with great sophistication on this complex process of splitting between human being and person, although coming to different conclusions from mine, is Y. Thomas, in "Le Sujet de droit, la personne et la nature," *Le Débat*, 100 (May–August 1998), pp. 85–107, and in "Le Sujet concret et sa personne. Essai d'histoire juridique rétrospective," in O. Cayla and Y. Thomas, *Du droit de ne pas naître*, Gallimard: Paris 2002, pp. 91–170.

17 Hans Kelsen, *Pure Theory of Law*, trans. Max Knight, University of California Press: Berkeley, Los Angeles, London 1978, p. 174.

18 Thomas Hobbes, *Leviathan*, in Thomas Hobbes, *The English Works*, vol. 3, John Bohn: London 1829–45, p. 158.

19 Ibid., p. 147.

20 Ibid., p. 150.

21 See F. Lessay, "Le Vocabulaire de la personne," in Y. C. Zarka (ed.), *Hobbes et son vocabulaire*, Paris 1992, pp. 155–86. On this topic, see the wide-ranging and well-documented work by A. Amendola, *Il sovrano e la maschera. Saggio sul concetto di persona in Thomas Hobbes*, Naples 1998.

22 T. Hobbes, *Leviathan*, p. 260.

23 Ibid., pp. 226ff.

24 Ibid., pp. 157–8.

25 J. Maritain, *The Rights of Man and Natural Law*, Gordian Press: New York 1971, p. 55.

26 Ibid., p. 138.

27 I am referring to Martin Heidegger, "Brief über den 'Humanismus,'" in *Wegmarken*, in *Gesamtausgabe*, Frankfurt am Main 1978, vol. 9; English version "Letter on Humanism," in *Basic Writings*, HarperCollins: New York 1993, pp. 213–66.

28 See Michel Foucault's works on this topic, especially *Naissance de la biopolitique. Cours au Collège de France 1978–1979*, Paris 2004; English version *The Birth of Biopolitics: Lectures at the Collège de*

*France, 1978–1979*, trans. Graham Burchell, Palgrave Macmillan: New York 2008.

29  See Roberto Esposito, "Totalitarismo o biopolitica? Per un'interpretazione filosofica del Novecento," in *Micromega*, 5, 2006, pp. 57–66.

30  Jürgen Habermas presents a similar argument coming from a different position, in *Die Zukunft der menschlichen Natur. Auf dem Weg zu einer liberalen Eugenik?*, Frankfurt am Main 2001; English version *The Future of Human Nature*, Polity: Cambridge 2003.

31  J. Locke, *Two Treatises of Government*, Simon and Schuster: New York 1970, p. 134.

32  John Stuart Mill, *On Liberty*, Bobbs-Merrill: Indianapolis 1956, p. 13.

33  On the relationship between body, person and thing, see I. Arnaux, *Les Droits de l'être humain sur son corps*, Bordeaux 1994, pp. 79ff.

34  On this issue, see the book by B. Edelman, *La Personne en danger*, Paris 1999, pp. 289–304.

35  B. Lemennicier, "Le Corps humain: propriété de l'état ou propriété de soi?" *Droits*, 13, 1991, p. 118.

36  See once again Edelman, *La Personne en danger*, pp. 305–22.

37  G. Fornero's *Bioetica cattolica e bioetica laica*, Milan 2005, provides a useful overview of the relationship between the various schools of bioethics.

38  Peter Singer, *Writings on an Ethical Life*, HarperCollins: New York 2000, p. 127.

39  Hugo Tristram Engelhardt, *The Foundations of Bioethics*, Oxford University Press: New York 1986, p. 157.

40  Singer, *Writings on an Ethical Life*, p. 193.

41  Ibid., p. 162.

42  Ibid., pp. 201–8.

43  Simone Weil, "Human Personality," in *Simone Weil: An Anthology*, ed. by Sian Miles, Grove Press: New York 1986, p. 62.

44  Ibid., p. 64.

45  Ibid., p. 61.

46  Ibid., p. 64.

47  Ibid., p. 54.

48  Ibid., pp. 55–6.

49  For the entire evolution of Simone Weil's thought, including the relationship between biological life and supernatural life, see the innovative, insightful book by A. Putin, *Un'intima estraneità*, Rome 2006.

50  S. Weil, "Human personality," pp. 57–8.

## Notes to Chapter 3

1   Émile Benveniste, "La Nature des pronoms (1956)," in Émile Benveniste, *Problèmes de linguistique générale*, Paris 1966; English version "The Nature of Pronouns," in Émile Benveniste, *Problems in General Linguistics*, trans. Mary Elizabeth Meek, University of Miami Press: Coral Gables, FL 1978, pp. 217–22, at p. 218.

2   Jacques Lacan, *Le Séminaire*, vol. 3: *Les Psychoses*, Paris 1981, p. 323; English version *The Seminar of Jacques Lacan*, Book 3: *The Psychoses*, trans. R. Grigg, W. W. Norton: New York 1993, p. 287.

3   Émile Benveniste, "Structure des relations de personne dans le verbe," in *Problèmes de linguistique générale*, vol. 1, Paris, 1976, pp. 225–36; English version "Relationships of Person in the Verb," in Paul Cobley (ed.), *The Communication Theory Reader*, Routledge: New York 1996, p. 323.

4   Ibid., p. 325.

5   Ibid.

6   Ibid., p. 328.

7   Ibid., p. 330.

8   Georg Simmel, *Soziologie*, Berlin 1908, pp. 90ff.; English version *The Sociology of Georg Simmel*, trans. Kurt H. Wolff, Free Press: Glencoe, IL 1950.

9   Alexandre Kojève, *Esquisse d'une phénoménologie du Droit*, Paris 1982; English version *Outline of a Phenomenology of Right*, trans. Bryan-Paul Frost and Robert Howse, Rowman & Littlefield: Lanham, MD 2000, p. 79.

10  On the relationship between Kojève and Schmitt, see G. Barberis, *Il regno della libertà. Diritto, politica e storia nel pensiero di Alexandre Kojève*, Naples 2003, as well as A. Gnoli's commentary at the end of Kojève's *Il silenzio della tirannide*, Milan 2004, pp. 253–67. More generally on Kojève's work, see M. Vegetti, *La fine della storia. Saggio sul pensiero di A. Kojève*, Milan 1999. On the figure of the third in the law, also in relation to Kojève, see B. Romano, *Ragione giuridica e terzietà nella relazione*, Rome 1998; also by B. Romano, *Sulla trasformazione della terzietà giuridica*, Turin 2006.

11  Carl Schmitt, "Der Begriff des Politischen," *Archiv für Sozialwissenschaft und Sozialpolitik*, 58 (1); English version *The Concept of the Political*, trans. George Schwab, Rutgers University Press: New Brunswick, NJ, 1976, p. 27. On the 'impossible' role of the third in politics, see also P. P. Portinaio, *Il terzo*, Milan 1986.

12  Kojève, *Outline of a Phenomenology of Right*, p. 216.

13   Ibid., p. 217.
14   Ibid., p. 88.
15   Ibid., p. 91.
16   Ibid., p. 94.
17   Alexandre Kojève, *Introduction à la lecture de Hegel*, Paris 1979, p. 434; English version *Introduction to the Reading of Hegel*, trans. Raymond Queneau, Cornell University Press: Princeton, NJ 1980, p. 158.
18   Quotation translated from the Italian edition of Kojève's *Outline of a Phenomenology of Right*: A. Kojève, *Linee di una fenomenologia del diritto*, ed. by F. D'Agostino, Milan 1989, p. 518.
19   Giorgio Agamben, by different routes, also reached the same conclusion. See his *L'aperto. L'uomo e l'animale*, Turin 2002, pp. 12–20; English version *The Open: Man and Animal*, Stanford University Press: Stanford, CA 2004.
20   V. Jankélévitch, *Traité des vertus*, vol. 2: *Les Vertus et l'amour*, Flammarion: Paris 1986, p. 113.
21   Ibid.
22   An article by V. Vitiello places him on a similar theoretical horizon, but with different arguments. See Vitiello's "TU. La metafisica della seconda persona," *Hermeneutica*, 34–7, 2004, pp. 9–37.
23   Jankélévitch, *Traité des vertus*, p. 111.
24   Ibid., p. 127.
25   Ibid., pp. 127–8.
26   Ibid., p. 114.
27   On the relationship between music and silence, see the powerful introductory essay by E. Lisciani-Petrini to the Italian edition of Victor Jankélévitch's *La musica e l'ineffabile*, Milan 1998 (French original *La Musique et l'ineffable*, Paris 1961).
28   Jankélévitch, *Traité des vertus*, p. 115.
29   Ibid., p. 126.
30   Ibid., p. 115.
31   Ibid., p. 131.
32   Emmanuel Levinas, "La Trace de l'autre," in Emmanuel Levinas, *En découvrant l'existence avec Husserl et Heidegger*, Paris 1967; English version "The Trace of the Other," trans. Alphonso Lingis, in Mark C. Taylor (ed.), *Deconstruction in Context: Literature and Philosophy*, University of Chicago Press: Chicago 1982, pp. 345–59, at p. 356.
33   See also Emmanuel Levinas, *Noms propres*, Montpellier 1976; English version *Proper Names*, trans. Michael B. Smith, Athlone Press: London 1996, pp. 17–35.

34 Emmanuel Levinas, *Totalité et infini. Essai sur l'exteriorité*, The Hague 1961; English version *Totality and Infinity*, Kluwer Academic Publishers: Dordrecht, The Netherlands 1991, p. 73.

35 Translator's note: from the third-person Latin pronoun *ille*, meaning roughly 'that one over there.'

36 Emmanuel Levinas, *Autrement qu'être ou au-delà de l'essence*, The Hague 1974; English version *Otherwise than Being or Beyond Essence*, trans. Alphonso Lingis, Dusquesne University Press: Pittsburgh, PA 1998, p. 157.

37 Emmanuel Levinas, "Le Moi et la totalité" [1954], in Emmanuel Levinas, *Entre nous. Essai sur le penser-à-l'autre*, Paris 1991, pp. 22–48; English version "The *I* and the Totality," in Emmanuel Levinas, *Entre nous: Thinking-of-the-Other*, trans. Michael B. Smith and Barbara Harshav, Columbia University Press: New York 1998, pp. 13–38.

38 Levinas, *Otherwise than Being*, p. 159.

39 For more in this line of reasoning, see Jacques Derrida, *Adieu à Emmanuel Levinas*, Paris 1977; English version *Adieu to Emmanuel Levinas*, trans. Pascale-Anne Brault and Michael Naas, Stanford University Press: Stanford, CA 1999.

40 Levinas, "The *I* and the Totality," p. 23.

41 Emmanuel Levinas, "Philosophy, Justice and Love," in Emmanuel Levinas, *Entre nous: Thinking-of-the-Other*, trans. Michael B. Smith and Barbara Harshav, Columbia University Press: New York 1998, pp. 103–22, at p. 108.

42 Levinas, *Otherwise than Being*, p. 159.

43 Ibid., p. 157.

44 Ibid.

45 Emmanuel Levinas, "Paix et proximité," in *Emmanuel Levinas*, ed. by J. Rolland, Paris 1984, p. 345; English version "Peace and Proximity," in *Emmanuel Levinas: Basic Philosophical Writings*, trans. Peter Atterton and Simon Critchley, ed. by Adriaan T. Peperzak, Simon Critchley, and Robert Bernasconi, Indiana University Press: Bloomington 1996, pp. 161–70, at p. 168.

46 M. Blanchot, *L'Entretien infini*, Paris 1969; English version *The Infinite Conversation*, trans. Susan Hanson, University of Minnesota Press: Minneapolis and London 1993, p. 52.

47 See Blanchot, *Infinite Conversation*, pp. 73ff.

48 Ibid., p. 70.

49 See the important book on this topic by M. Zarader, *L'Être et le neutre. À partir de Maurice Blanchot*, Paris 2001; see also F. Garritano, *Sul neutro. Saggio su Maurice Blanchot*, Florence 1992,

and P. Mesnard, *Maurice Blanchot. Le sujet de l'engagement*, Paris 1996. Translator's note: the Latin adjective *neuter* ('neither'/'neutral') is a compound of the pronoun *uter(que)* ('which of the two?'/'each of the two'/'both') and the negative particle *ne*.

50   Blanchot, *Infinite Conversation*, p. 72.

51   Maurice Blanchot, *Le Pas au-delà*, Gallimard: Paris 1973, p. 53; English version *The Step Not Beyond*, trans. Lycette Nelson, State University of New York Press: Albany 1992, p. 36.

52   Blanchot, *Infinite Conversation*, p. 299.

53   Ibid., p. 312.

54   Ibid., p. 299.

55   Emmanuel Levinas, *De l'existence à l'existant*, Paris 1978; English version *Existence and Existents*, trans. Alfonso Lingis, Kluwer Academic Press: Dordrecht, Boston, and London 1988, p. 57.

56   Ibid., p. 64.

57   Maurice Blanchot, *Écrits politiques. Guerre d'Algérie, Mai 68, etc. 1958–1993*, Paris 2003; English version *Political Writings, 1953–1993*, trans. Zakir Paul, Fordham University Press: Bronx, NY 2010, p. 150.

58   Maurice Blanchot, *The Space of Literature*, trans. Ann Smock, University of Nebraska Press: Lincoln 1989, p. 33.

59   Blanchot, *Infinite Conversation*, p. 381.

60   Ibid.

61   Ibid, p. 384.

62   Blanchot, *Political Writings*, p. 7.

63   Ibid., p. 36.

64   Ibid., p. 165.

65   Ibid., p. 57.

66   Ibid., p. 58.

67   Ibid., p. 85.

68   Maurice Blanchot, *Michel Foucault tel que je l'imagine*, Paris 1986; English version "Michel Foucault as I Imagine Him," in *Foucault–Blanchot*, trans. Jeffrey Mehlman and Brian Massumi, Zone Books: New York 1987, pp. 61–109, at p. 63.

69   Ibid., p. 64. Translator's note: the English translation has been slightly adapted.

70   G. Deleuze, *Pourparler*, Paris 1990; English version: *Negotiations, 1972–1990*, trans. Martin Joughin, Columbia University Press: New York 1990, p. 115.

71   Ibid., p. 108.

72   M. Foucault, *L'Archéologie du savoir*, Paris 1969; English version *The Archaeology of Knowledge*, trans. A. M. Sheridan Smith, Routledge: Abingdon, Oxon, UK 2005, p. 138.

73 On Foucault's literary writings, see J. Revel, *Foucault, le parole e i poteri*, Rome 1996. More generally, on his philosophical lexicon, see also E. Castro, *El vocabulario de Michel Foucault*, Buenos Aires 2004.

74 M. Foucault, "La Penseé du dehors," in M. Foucault, *Dits et écrits*, vol. 1: *1954–1975*, Paris 2001; English version "The Thought of the Outside," in *Essential Works of Foucault 1954–1984*, vol. 2: *Aesthetics, Method, and Epistemology*, ed. by Paul Rabinow, trans. Robert J. Hurley, New Press: New York 1998, pp. 147–69, at p. 165.

75 Foucault, "What Is an Author?" in *The Essential Works of Foucault, 1954–1984*, vol. 1: *Ethics*, ed. by Paul Rabinow and Nikolas Rose, New Press: New York, 2003, p. 206.

76 Gilles Deleuze, *Foucault*, Paris 1986; English version *Foucault*, trans. Seán Hand, Continuum: London 1999, p. 72.

77 Ibid., p. 96.

78 Michel Foucault, *Les Mots et les choses*, Paris 1967; English version *The Order of Things*, Vintage Books: New York 1994, p. 297.

79 Ibid., pp. 324–5.

80 Deleuze, *Foucault*, p. 100.

81 Michel Foucault, *La Volonté de savoir*, Paris 1976; English version *The Will to Knowledge*, vol. 1: *History of Sexuality*, trans. Robert Hurley, Penguin Books: London 1998, p. 143.

82 Ibid., p. 144.

83 Ibid., pp. 144–5.

84 Ibid., p. 145.

85 Deleuze, *Foucault*, p. 79.

86 M. Foucault, "La Vie des hommes infâmes," in M. Foucault, *Écrits*, vol. 3; English version "Lives of Infamous Men," in James D. Faubion (ed.), *Power: Essential Works of Foucault*, vol. 3, New Press: New York 2003, pp. 157–75, at pp. 161, 159, and 163.

87 Gilles Deleuze, *Logique du sens*, Paris 1969; English version *Logic of Sense*, Continuum: London 2004, p. 171.

88 Gilles Deleuze and Félix Guattari, *L'Anti-Oedipe. Capitalisme et schizophrénie*, vol. 1, Paris 1972; English version *Anti-Oedipus: Capitalism and Schizophrenia*, vol. 1, Continuum: London 2004, p. 80.

89 Gilles Deleuze, *Critique et clinique*, Paris 1993; English version *Essays Clinical and Critical*, trans. Daniel W. Smith and Michael A. Greco, Verso: London and New York 1998, p. 3.

90 Ibid., p. 5.

91 Gilles Deleuze, "L'Immanence: une vie ...," *Philosophie*, 47, September 1995, pp. 3–7; English version "Immanence: A Life," in

Gilles Deleuze, *Pure Immanence: Essays on A Life*, trans. Anne Boyman, Zone Books: New York 2001, pp. 25–33.

92    In this regard, see R. Scherer, "Homo tantum. L'impersonnel: une politique," in E. Alliez (ed.), *Gilles Deleuze. Une vie philosophique*, Le Plessis-Robinson 1998, pp. 25–42. Roberto Ciccarelli's *Immanenza. Filosofia, diritto e politica della vita dal XIX al XX secolo*, Il Mulino: Bologna 2009 presents a broad genealogy of thought on immanence, taking Deleuze as his departure point.

93    Gilles Deleuze and Felix Guattari, *Mille plateaux. Schizophrenia et capitalisme*, Paris 1980; English version *A Thousand Plateaus. Capitalism and Schizophrenia*, University of Minnesota Press, Minneapolis, MN and London 1987, p. 265. For a political reading of *A Thousand Plateaus*, see the incisive essay by Michael Hardt, "La Société mondiale de contrôle," in *Gilles Deleuze. Une vie philosophique*, ed. by E. Alliez, Le Plessis-Robinson 1998, pp. 359–75.

94    Deleuze and Guattari, *A Thousand Plateaus*, pp. 239–40.

95    Ibid., p. 241.

# Index